# *Interactive*
# BIBLE
# Bulletin Boards

## Winter

by Susan Julio
and
Cindy Schooler

**These pages may be copied.**

**Permission is granted** to the buyer of this book to reproduce, duplicate or photocopy these student materials for use with pupils in Sunday school or Bible teaching classes.

Rainbow Publishers

Rainbow Publishers • P.O. Box 261129 • San Diego, CA 92196

# ✳ Dedication ✳

To my church family at the Meadowbrook Church of God. Thanks for the encouraging words, well wishes and especially your prayers. You really know how to love a gal! —C.S.

INTERACTIVE BIBLE BULLETIN BOARDS FOR WINTER
©1998 by Rainbow Publishers
ISBN 1-885358-33-4

Rainbow Publishers
P.O. Box 261129
San Diego, CA 92196

Illustrator: Joel Ryan
Editor: Christy Allen
Design: Stray Cat Studio, San Diego, CA

Scriptures are from the *Holy Bible: New International Version* (North American Edition), copyright ©1973, 1978, 1984 by the International Bible Society. Used by permission of Zondervan Bible Publishers.

*Printed in the United States of America*

# Interactive BIBLE Bulletin Boards

## ✻ Contents ✻

# Interactive BIBLE Bulletin Boards

## ✴ Introduction ✴

Bulletin boards can be fun, involve your students and use easy-to-find supplies, plus look great and offer solid Bible-teaching. That's why *Interactive Bible Bulletin Boards* was created: to provide the materials you need to make bulletin boards that you can use to teach about God. Each of the four seasonal books in the *Interactive Bulletin Board* series contains 13 bulletin boards for preschoolers and 13 bulletin boards for elementary-age kids. Just one book has enough bulletin board patterns and ideas for your church's entire children's department!

The best part about this book is that all of the bulletin boards either involve the children in creating them—allowing you more time to spend on teaching—or involve them with learning manipulatives that you display. Either way, you will quickly construct exciting bulletin boards that reach kids.

Each bulletin board is a lesson, including:

| | |
|---|---|
| ✴ Plan | the lesson's objective |
| ✴ Memorize | an age-based memory verse |
| ✴ Gather | a supply list |
| ✴ Prepare | pre-class tasks for you to complete |
| ✴ Create | step-by-step instructions |
| ✴ Teach | ideas to extend the lesson |

You will also find all of the patterns for each bulletin board, plus borders and lettering to complete the board's look. Tips on pages 6-9 will help you make the most of the book, as well as your supplies and creativity.

The bulletin boards in this book are unique. They were created out of a desire to see children using the bulletin board as an extension to teaching a biblical concept. These boards say, "Yes, please touch" in a world that tells children, "No, don't touch." The children in your classroom will love the new experience you are about to give them.

# ✳ How to Create Beautiful Bulletin Boards Using the Materials in This Book ✳

Each of the 26 Bible-teaching, interactive bulletin boards in this book contains complete instructions, patterns, lettering and borders to put the bulletin board together, plus teaching hints to use the board with your class. The following pages will offer you ideas for your bulletin boards and explain how to best use the book.

## ✳ Backgrounds

Each bulletin board in this book includes suggestions for background colors—most people use poster paper or construction paper. You may want to select a background that will work with board designs you will use throughout the season. Also, feel free to experiment with materials of your choice to add background interest, such as:

* Textured fabrics: felt, flannel, burlap, fur, cheesecloth
* Paper or plastic tablecloths
* Gift wrap
* Cotton batting
* Newspaper
* Brown paper bags crumpled and then flattened
* Maps
* Crepe paper
* Colored tissue paper
* Wallpaper
* Self-stick plastic in colors or patterns
* Shelf paper
* Colorful corrugated paper available from school supply stores
* Poster board on which figures may be permanently attached

## ✳ Making Bulletin Boards Three-Dimensional

Although bulletin boards are normally flat, there are many imaginative ways to add a three-dimensional effect to them. Many of the bulletin boards in this book already include ideas for three-dimensional effects, but there are others you may want to try:

* Place cork, cardboard or foam behind figures or letters.
* Attach large figures to the bulletin board by curving them slightly outward from the board.
* Glue or attach three-dimensional objects such as cotton balls, pieces of wood, twigs, nature items, feathers, yarn, toys, small clothing objects (like scarves and mittens), balloons, artificial flowers or leaves, chenille wire, fabric, corrugated paper, sandpaper, crumpled aluminum foil or grocery bags, rope, plastic drinking straws—the list can go on and on!

* "Stuff" figures by putting crumpled newspaper or paper towels behind the figures before attaching them to the bulletin board.

* Flowers may be made from individual egg carton sections by cutting off the sections and painting, coloring or decorating them as desired.

* Heavy objects may be mounted in the following way: Cut two or more strips of bias binding tape or ribbon (available from fabric stores). Securely staple one end of the bias tape to the bulletin board, place around the item to be mounted and staple the other end (above the object) to the bulletin board so the object hangs securely on the bias tape strips.

# *Lettering

This book includes full-sized lettering which is intended to be used on the bulletin boards that you create. To use the lettering, you may do any of the following:

* Trace the lettering onto colored construction paper, cut out each letter and mount them individually on the bulletin board.

* Duplicate the lettering onto any paper. Then place that page over the sheet of paper out of which you want to cut the letters. Cut through both sheets using scissors or a craft knife. Mount the letters individually on the bulletin board.

* Duplicate the lettering onto white paper and color in the letters with markers.

* Duplicate the lettering onto white or colored paper. Cut the words apart and mount each word on the bulletin board in strip form.

* Trace the lettering onto paper of any color using colored markers. Cut out the individual letters or cut apart the words and use them in strip form.

* Cut the individual letters out of two colors of paper at once. When mounting the letters on the bulletin board, lay one color on top of the other and offset the bottom letter slightly so it creates a shadow effect.

Attractive lettering can also be made by cutting letters out of wallpaper, fabrics, felt, self-stick plastic in colors and patterns, gift wrap, grocery bags, newspapers and other materials. For a professional look, outline letters with a dark marker for a neat edge and good contrast. Always try to use dark colors for lettering, unless the background requires a contrasting color.

Textures may be used for lettering also, either by cutting the letters out of textured materials or by gluing on glitter, sequins, straw, twigs, yarn, rope, lace, craft sticks, chenille wire or other materials.

To mount the letters flat, staple them to the board, use double-sided tape or roll a small piece of tape to make it double-sided. Always put the tape under the letter so it does not show.

Stagger the letters, arch them, dip them or make them look like stair steps or a wave by variegating one letter up and one letter down. Be a non-conformist when it comes to letter placement! Curve your lettering around the board, place your title down one side or across the bottom. Your title doesn't always have to be across the top of the bulletin board.

## ✳ Duplicating Patterns and Lettering

All patterns, lettering and borders in this book may be used right out of the book or traced, enlarged, reduced, duplicated or photocopied to make your bulletin board.

The easiest way to duplicate the materials in this book is to use a copy machine to simply copy the patterns, lettering or borders onto white or colored copy machine paper. For a nominal price you can copy onto colored paper at most copy centers. Construction paper works well in some copy machines.

You may also trace the materials in this book onto white or colored paper by holding the page you wish to trace up to a window or by using carbon paper.

Another way to enlarge items is with an overhead projector. Trace the items you wish to enlarge onto a transparency sheet, then project the image onto a sheet of paper attached to a wall. Adjust the projector until the image is the size you desire and trace the image onto the paper.

## ✳ Mounting Materials onto Your Bulletin Board

It is important that all materials stay securely on your bulletin board until you wish to take them down. This book does not specify how to mount most materials so you may choose the method that works best for your situation.

Stapling materials directly to the bulletin board is the most secure method of mounting most materials and the staples are virtually unnoticeable. Be sure to have a staple remover handy both when you are creating the board and when you are taking it down.

Staples are much better for bulletin boards for small children as it is quite difficult to pull a staple out of a bulletin board, unlike push pins and tacks. Make certain that no loose staples are left on the floor after you finish working on the bulletin board.

Pins may be used if you wish to support the materials rather than make holes. Double-sided tape, or tape rolled to make it double-sided, is also effective. For heavier materials, use carpet tape or packing tape.

## ✳ How to Make Your Bulletin Boards Durable and Reusable

Cover both sides of your bulletin board figures—especially those that will be manipulated by the children—with self-stick plastic. Cut around the figures, leaving a ¼" edge of plastic. (If one figure is made up of several parts, put the parts together before covering with plastic.) You may also glue figures to colored construction paper and cut around them, leaving a narrow border of construction paper.

Also laminate the captions and borders to use again. Take a picture of your completed bulletin board for future color references and diagrams. Glue the developed picture to the outside of a large manila envelope and store the laminated pieces of the bulletin board inside.

# ✳ Teaching with the Bulletin Boards

Each of the bulletin boards in this book includes a suggested memory verse and teaching tips to help you use the bulletin boards to teach important biblical concepts to children.

On those that are designed for the children to assist you in the board's creation, you will find that the students delight in helping and seeing their work on the board. The boards that you create for the children to use in learning will also intrigue and engage them. Almost all of the boards that the children will help you to create require scissors and a few other easy-to-obtain items. A list of materials is included with each board.

Since the titles for these bulletin boards were chosen to encourage a learning concept, they are important to the overall interaction with the bulletin board. The first week that each new bulletin board is displayed, read the titles aloud to the children—especially preschoolers—and explain what it means. Also, show the children how to interact with the board. If you take time at the beginning of the class to introduce the board, you won't have as many individual questions to answer during your lesson. Memory verses were purposely not included on most of the finished bulletin boards for preschoolers since they cannot read, but your continued verbal repetition of the verses will make them familiar to the students.

Bulletin boards are great teaching tools. Besides being obvious colorful additions to a classroom, they can also be used in the following ways:

- ✳ Reinforce the lesson
- ✳ Improve fine motor skills
- ✳ Serve as focal point of classroom
- ✳ Review the previous week's lesson
- ✳ Introduce new topics
- ✳ Encourage new skills (such as following a maze, turning wheels, opening flaps, etc.)
- ✳ Keep and encourage attendance
- ✳ Enhance self-image by displaying work
- ✳ Encourage interaction with other children

These bulletin boards are unique because they encourage the children to interact with them in some way. Whether the board displays their own work, helps record attendance or allows them to move objects around, the children are encouraged to interact with the bulletin board each time they come into the classroom.

# ✳ Visitors

Be sure to create a few extras of each child-specific item so that visitors will have copies. Your new students will feel more welcome if they know you are prepared for them.

# ✳ A Special Note to Preschool Teachers

The best way to organize a classroom for toddlers is down on your knees! Remember that these are little people, so make sure all of your displays are at their eye level. Lower the bulletin board if possible. Make sure the children can easily reach the interactive activities you create with this book.

## ✳ Borders

Borders are the frame of your bulletin board. Just as you carefully choose an appropriate frame for a picture on the wall, you should choose a border that will enhance your bulletin board. Several border patterns are provided on the following pages for use with selected bulletin boards in this book.

The easiest method for creating and duplicating borders is decribed below. Simply measure the top, bottom and sides of your board (write down the measurements so you will have them the next time you are making a border). Then follow the directions for instant borders. Cut, fold and trace as many strips as you need for your board based on your measurements. You may use colored paper for the borders or copy the patterns onto white paper and have the children color them in with markers.

Glue or tape the border lengths together. Use double-faced tape to attach the border directly to the frame, or staple the border to the edge of the bulletin board. Roll the border to store for future use.

Attractive borders may also be made with the following materials:

* Artificial flowers, leaves or nature items
* Rope or twine
* Braided yarn
* Wide gift wrap ribbon
* Corrugated borders available from school supply stores
* Twisted crepe paper streamers
* Christmas tree garland
* Aluminum foil (makes wonderful icicles!)

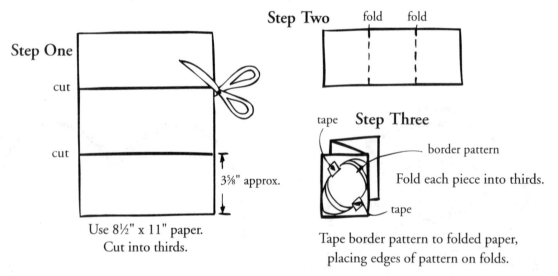

**Step One**

cut

cut

3⅝" approx.

Use 8½" x 11" paper.
Cut into thirds.

**Step Two**

fold    fold

**Step Three**

tape

border pattern

Fold each piece into thirds.

tape

Tape border pattern to folded paper,
placing edges of pattern on folds.

**Step Four**

Cut out pattern. Leave edges that touch folds uncut.

Borders will look
like this:

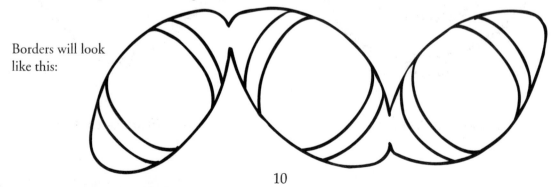

# ✳ Border Patterns ✳

coat border

crown border

dollar sign border

heart border

# ✳ Border Patterns ✳

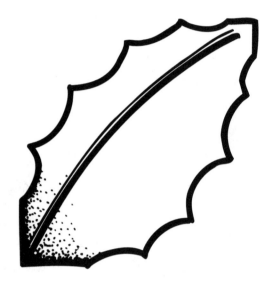

holly leaf border

log border

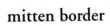

mitten border

olive leaf border

# ✳ Border Patterns ✳

shield border

star border

snowflake border

bear border

tree border

# Children Are A Gift From God

Children are a reward from him.
Psalm 127:3

## ✶ Plan

To show children that they are important to God.

## ✶ Memorize

*Children [are] a reward from him.* Psalm 127:3

## ✶ Gather

- pattern for lettering from pp. 15-16
- gift wrap
- boxes
- background paper, black
- ribbon, assorted colors
- chalk
- baby photographs of students

## ✶ Prepare

Duplicate the lettering and trace it onto gift wrap.

## ✶ Create

1. Cover the bulletin board with black background paper. Cut out the lettering and attach it to the board as shown. Post ribbon along the board's edges for a border.

2. Write the memory verse with chalk on the bottom of the board.

3. Wrap the tops of the boxes with gift wrap and add a ribbon for decoration.

4. Attach the bottoms of the boxes to the bulletin board, interiors facing out. Tape the baby photographs of the students inside the boxes. Cover the boxes with the wrapped lids.

## ✶ Teach

Have the students remove the lids and guess which classmate the baby in the box is. You may conduct the activity as a game by keeping points or allowing the children to individually test their knowledge. Add to the theme by reading the story of Jesus and the children from the Bible (Mark 10:13-16) or from a Bible story book.

Suggested Usage: Christmas

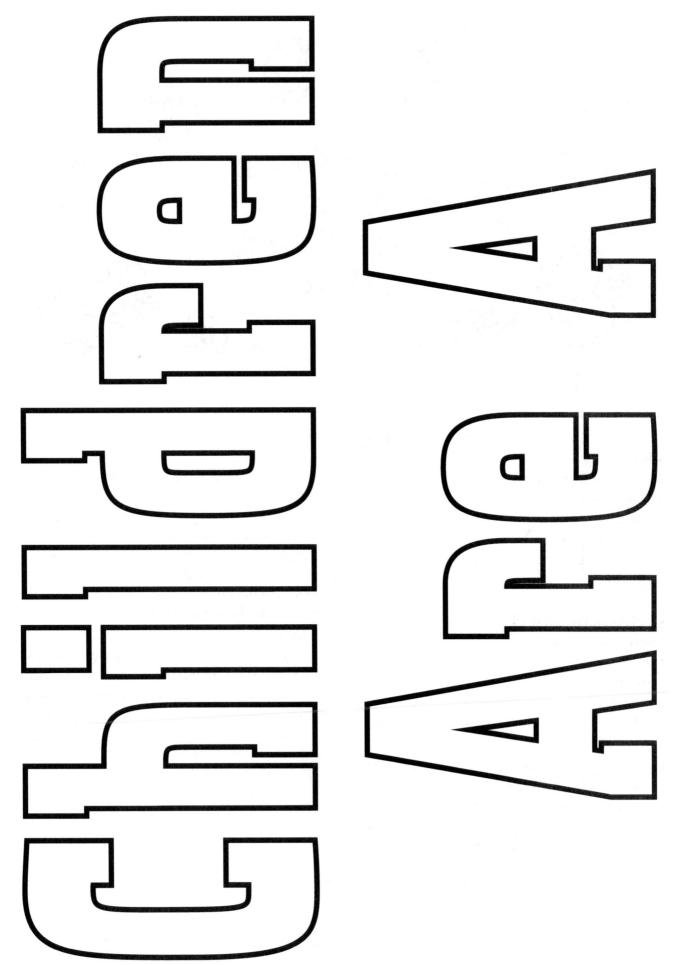

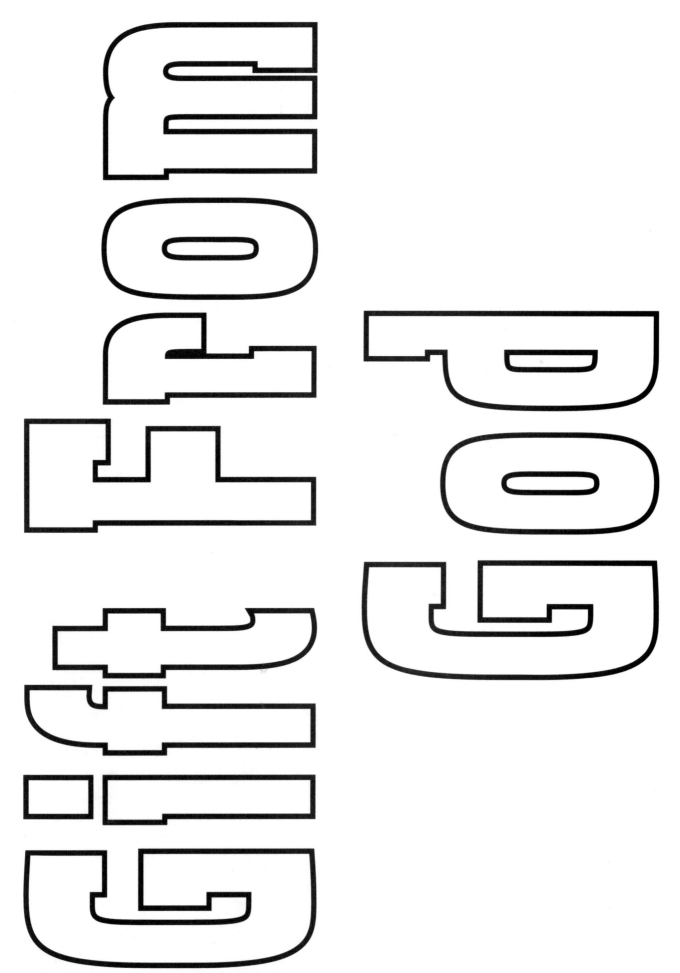

Gift From

God

# Crowns of Glory

*They do it to get a crown that will not last; but we do it to get a crown that will last forever.*
1 Corinthians 9:25

## ✱ Ages 6-10 ✱

### ✱ Plan
To learn that earthly riches are nothing compared to God's plan for us.

### ✱ Memorize
*They do it to get a crown that will not last; but we do it to get a crown that will last forever.*
1 Corinthians 9:25

### ✱ Gather
• pattern for lettering from p. 19
• pattern for crown from p. 18
• pattern for crown border from p. 11
• poster paper, black
• aluminum foil
• glue
• safety scissors
• glitter, gold or silver
• poster board
• construction paper, yellow
• faux jewels
• tissue paper

### ✱ Prepare
Duplicate the lettering and trace onto foil. Duplicate one crown per student on white paper.

### ✱ Create
1. Cover the bulletin board with black paper. Cut out the lettering and attach it to the board.

2. To make the border, cut and fold yellow paper according to the directions on page 10. Trace the crown border onto the folded paper and cut out the border. Post it around the edges of the board.

3. Use glue to "write" the Bible verse at the bottom of the board, then sprinkle the glue with glitter. Allow time for the glue to dry before the students arrive.

4. Distribute the crowns and poster board to the students. Have them cut out and trace the crowns onto poster board, then cut those out.

5. Show how to cover the crown with aluminum foil. Allow the students to glue faux jewels (found in craft stores), glitter or bits of colored tissue paper on their crowns.

6. Attach the crowns to the bulletin board.

### ✱ Teach
You can also use the pattern to make wearable crowns. Simply use a hole punch on either side of the crown. Slip a length of yarn through the holes and tie on each child's head. Explain that this crown will not last long, just like the memory verse says material things in life will not last long. But if we know Jesus, our crowns of life will last forever!

Suggested Usage: Christmas or Epiphany

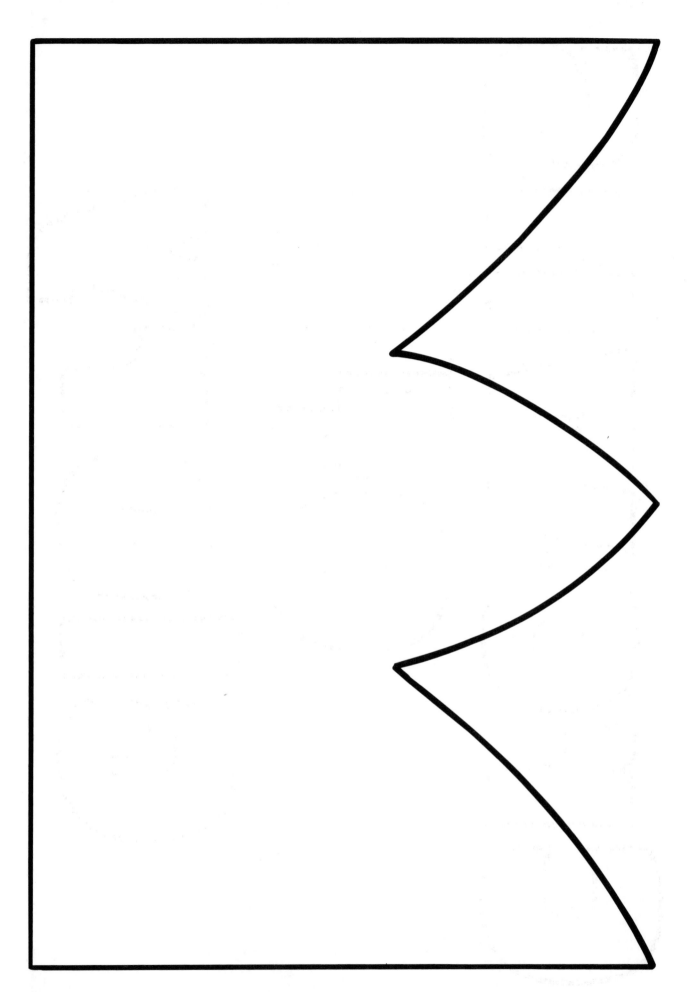

crowns

of

Glory

**Especially for Jesus**

## ✳ Plan
To learn that Jesus was the best gift of all.

## ✳ Memorize
*Your Father in heaven give[s] good gifts.*
Matthew 7:11

## ✳ Gather
- pattern for name tags from p. 21
- pattern for lettering from p. 22
- pattern for snowflake border from p. 13
- construction paper, white and black
- background paper or gift wrap, any color
- empty boxes, small
- bows and ribbon
- marker, black
- ribbon
- hole punch
- nativity scene
- ink pad, red

## ✳ Prepare
Duplicate the name tags on white paper and the lettering on black paper.

## ✳ Create
1. Attach the colored background paper to the bulletin board. Cut out and attach the lettering on the board.
2. Cut and fold strips of white paper according to the instant border directions on page 10. Trace the snowflake border on the folded paper and cut out. Staple the border around the board's edges.
3. Cover the empty boxes with gift wrap. Wrap the lid separately so that the lid can be removed without tearing the gift wrap.
4. Staple the bottoms of the boxes to the board (the box will extend from the board). Place the top of the box on its half that is stapled to the board.
5. Cut out the name tags. Fill in each tag with a child's name in black marker, or assist the children as they write their names.
6. Using the red ink pad, have the children make a thumb print on their name tag. Punch a hole in the tags and tie them dangling from the gifts.

## ✳ Teach
Ask, **Does anyone know why we give gifts at Christmas? It's because we are remembering that God gave us Jesus on the very first Christmas.** Show a nativity scene. **So every time we give a gift, we are sharing Jesus with that person, just like God shared His Son, Jesus, with us. Let's pray and thank God for His gift.** Lead in a short prayer. If desired, give each child a small gift to reinforce the act of giving as God gave Jesus to us.

Suggested Usage: Christmas

Especially
For : **Jesus**

From:

Especially
For : **Jesus**

From:

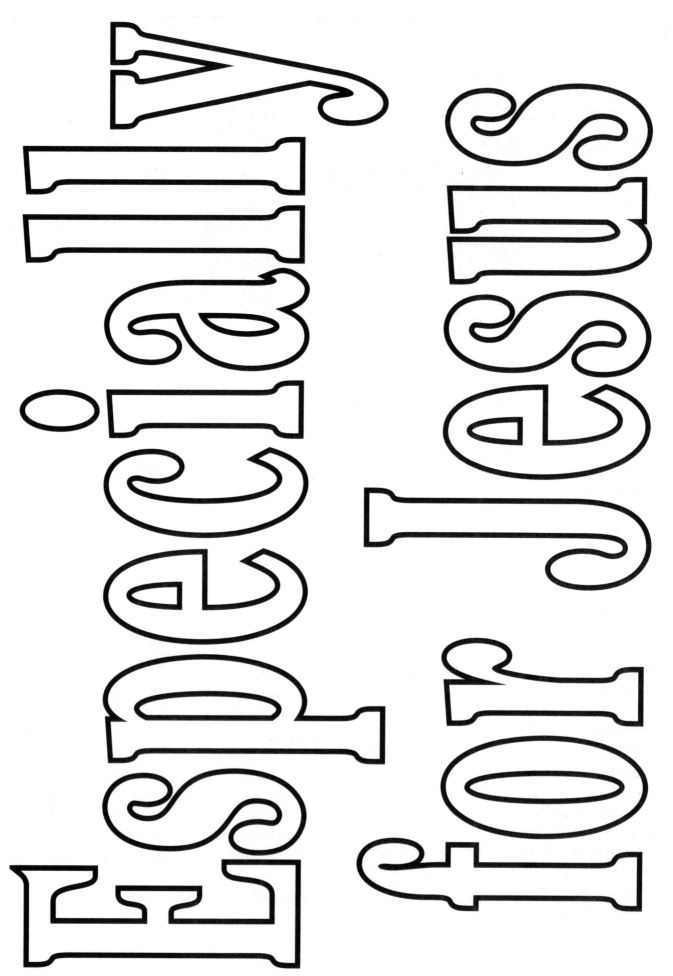

Especially for Jesus

He Is The Son Of God

## * Plan
To explain the birth of Jesus.

## * Memorize
*Give him the name Jesus.* Matthew 1:21

## * Gather
- patterns for nativity figures from pp. 24-28
- pattern for lettering from pp. 29-30
- pattern for star border from p. 13
- felt, green
- construction paper, yellow and brown
- glue
- paper, white
- sandpaper
- hay or raffia (optional)

## * Prepare
Duplicate the lettering on yellow construction paper.

## * Create
1. Attach the green felt for the background. Cut out the lettering and post it on the board.
2. Cut and fold strips of paper according to the instant border directions on page 10. Trace the star border pattern onto the folded paper and cut out the border. Staple the border around the board's edges.
3. Cut out a stable shape from brown construction paper as shown in the small illustration on p. 28 and attach it to the center of the board. Attach raffia, hay or construction paper along the roof.
4. Duplicate or cut out the nativity firgues and the star (enlarge, if desired). Color them but do not attach them to the board. Glue sandpaper to the back of each figure.
5. Each week, add nativity figures to the board and discuss their roles in announcing Jesus' birth. (Example: Week one: Add Mary and Joseph in the stable. Week two: The shepherds in the fields and the angels in the sky. Week three: Baby Jesus. Week four: The Wise Men and the star.)

## * Teach
Tell the story of Jesus' birth and allow the children to place the characters on the board as the story is told. After a few weeks of your telling the story, have the children tell the story themselves and place the characters on the board at the appropriate times.

Suggested Usage: Christmas

### To Make a Stable

1. Use brown paper, thin wood or woodgrain-like self-stick plastic.
2. Cut as shown at right.
3. Cover with raffia, shown bunched at right, which is available at craft stores. Or, be creative and design your own stable using twigs, paint or other materials.

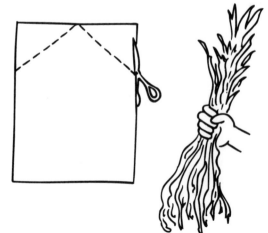

**His Light Shines**

**In Our Hearts**

## ✳ Plan
To teach the meaning of advent.

## ✳ Memorize
*God is light.* 1 John 1:5

## ✳ Gather
• patterns for candle, berries and holly from p. 32
• pattern for lettering from pp. 33-34
• pattern for heart border from p. 11
• poster paper, yellow
• construction paper, purple, pink, white, green and red
• felt, red
• marker, black
• Velcro
• safety scissors

## ✳ Prepare
Duplicate the lettering on red construction paper.

## ✳ Create
1. Attach the yellow paper to the bulletin board. Cut out and post the lettering.
2. Cut and fold strips of red paper according to the instant border directions on page 10. Trace the heart border onto the folded paper and cut out. Staple the border around the board's edges.
3. Trace the candle pattern, making three purple, one pink and one white candle. Cut out the candles. On each purple candle write one of the following: Waiting, Joy or Praise. On the pink candle, write Faith. Leave the white candle blank.

Post the candles on the board with the white candle in the center.
4. Trace the holly leaves on green paper and the berries on red paper. Allow the children to cut them out. (Don't worry about how "perfect" they look.) Post them at the bases of the candles.
5. Trace five flames on red felt. Attach pieces of Velcro to the backs of the flames and above the candles on the bulletin board.
6. Each week before Christmas, "light" a candle by attaching a flame to it. Since the children can move the flames, make sure you light the proper candle each week. The candles should be lit in this order: Waiting, Joy, Praise and Faith. The white candle should be the last lit. Each week, talk about what each candle represents in the Christmas story by reading the related scriptures (see below).

## ✳ Teach
On the last week of Advent allow the children to tell you about the candles. Since they cannot read, they may confuse the order in which they were lit, but that is not so important. The goal is for them to be able to tell you that the candles are named Waiting, Joy, Praise and Faith, and that each of these attributes is included in the Christmas story. Waiting—Isaiah 9:2, 6; Joy—Luke 2:9-11; Praise—Luke 2:13-14; and Faith—Galatians 3:23-26.

Suggested Usage: Advent

31

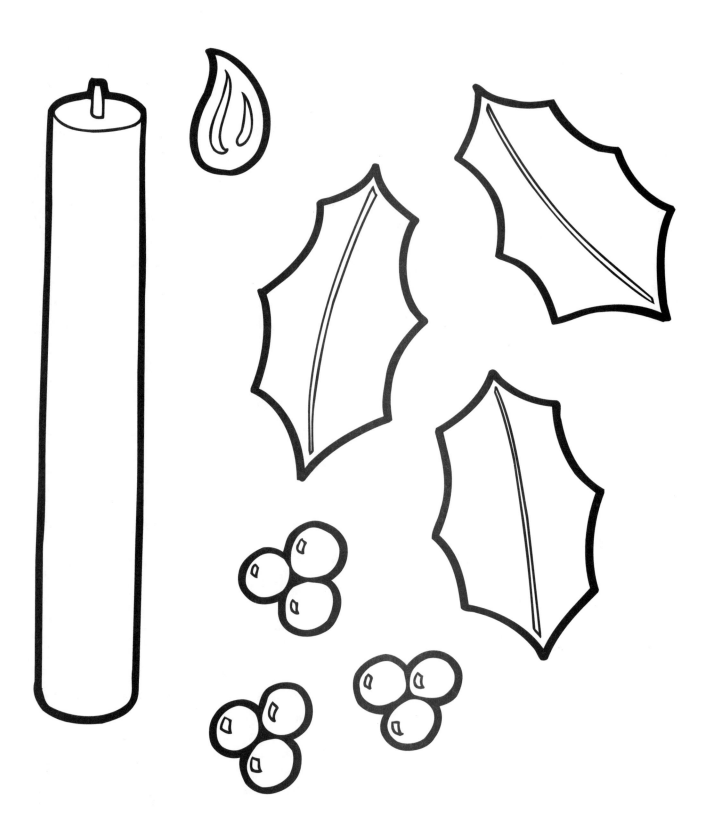

His Light Shines

In Our Hearts

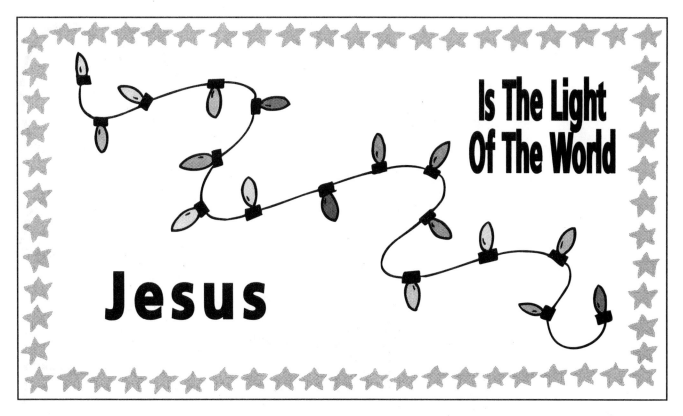

Jesus Is The Light Of The World

### ❋ Plan
To encourage attendance, and focus on Jesus' birth.

### ❋ Memorize
*He said, "I am the light of the world."* John 8:12

### ❋ Gather
- patterns for sockets and bulbs from pp. 36-37
- pattern for lettering from pp. 38-39
- pattern for star border from p. 13
- December calendar page
- background paper, white
- paper, white
- construction paper, various colors
- yarn, green
- marker, black

### ❋ Prepare
Duplicate the lettering on green construction paper, and a December calendar page on white paper.

### ❋ Create
1. Post the white background paper on the bulletin board. Cut out the lettering and attach it to the board as shown in the illustration.
2. Cut and fold strips of yellow construction paper according to the instant border directions on page 10. Trace the star border pattern onto the folded paper and cut out the border. Staple the border around the edges of the board.
3. Form a base string for the lights by attaching a long strand of green yarn in a wavy pattern on the board.
4. Trace and cut several sockets using the socket pattern and green construction paper. Attach them to the board on the yarn at appropriate intervals.
5. Make the light bulbs by tracing the pattern on various colors of construction paper or color them in. Cut out the bulbs, but do not staple them to the string.
6. Each week a child attends class, he or she will receive a light bulb. Help the child write his or her name on the bulb. Assist the child in stapling the light bulb to the string on the bulletin board. Be sure to supervise the use of the stapler, as this may be the first time your preschoolers have operated a stapler.

### ❋ Teach
Give each child a copy of a December calendar so they may continue the "counting" activity at home. Instruct the students to color one square on the calendar each day. When they reach day 25, it will be Christmas—the day we celebrate Jesus' birth!

Suggested Usage: Christmas

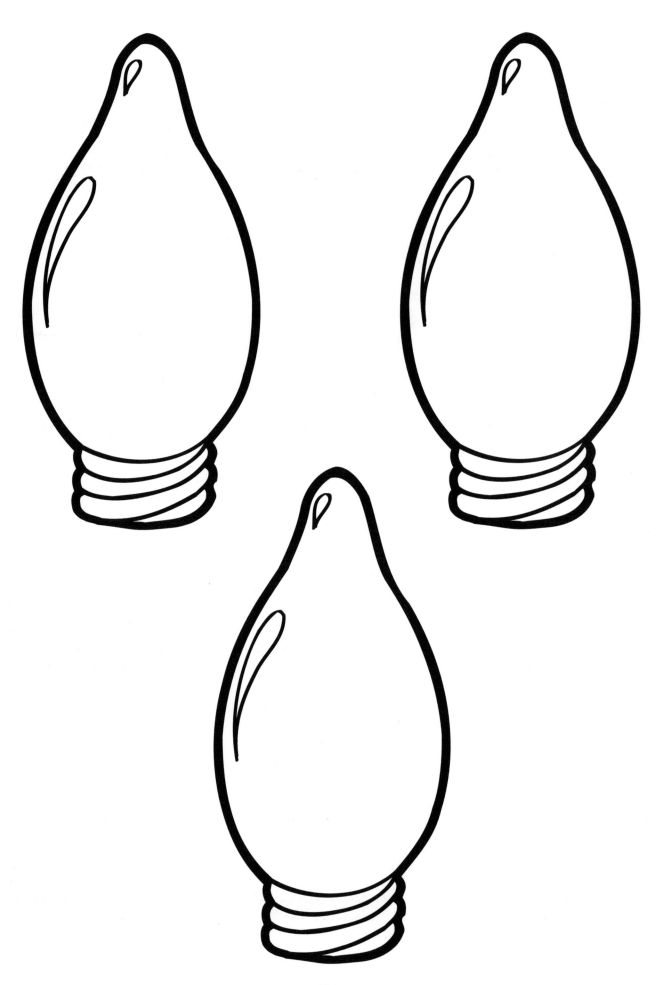

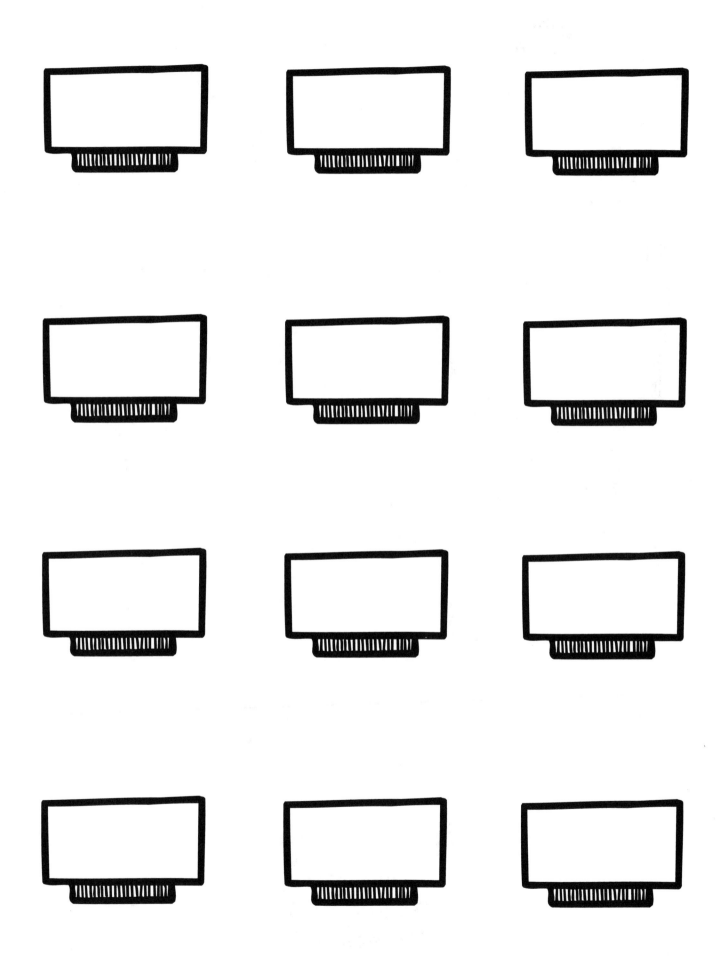

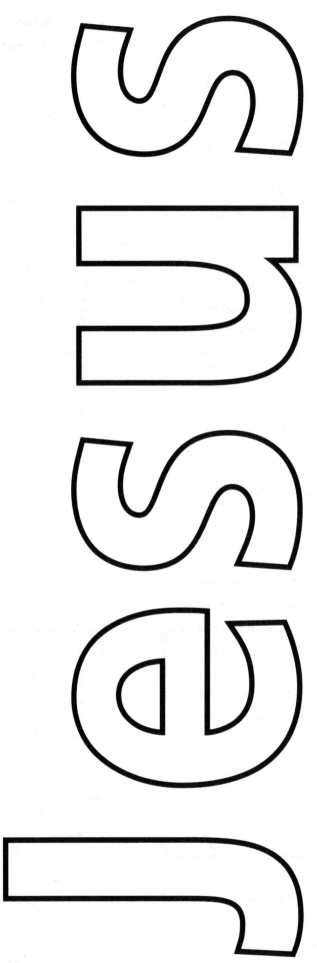

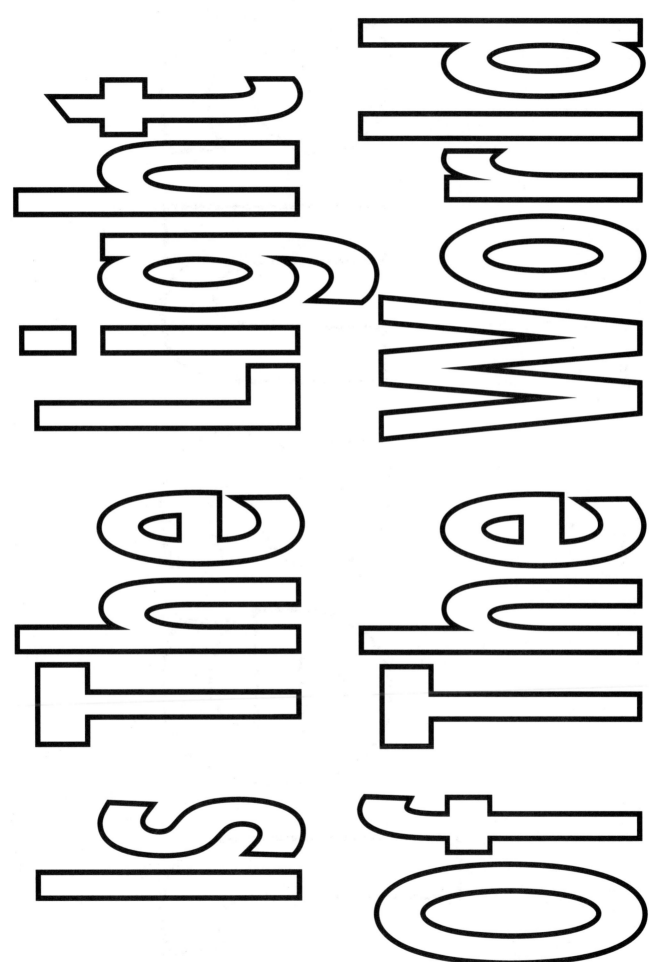

The Light Of The World

**Miracle Workers**

I can do everything through him who gives me strength.
Philippians 4:13

(Stockings labeled: ELIJAH, MOSES, JESUS, ELISHA)

## ✳ Ages 6-10 ✳

### ✳ Plan
To review miracles of the Bible.

### ✳ Memorize
*I can do everything through him who gives me strength.* Philippians 4:13

### ✳ Gather
- pattern for lettering from p. 44
- pattern for stocking and cane from pp. 42-43
- pattern for holly leaf border from p. 12
- poster paper, white
- construction paper, green, red, white and black
- rectangular sponge
- shallow dish or pie pan
- tempera paint, red
- markers, black and red
- glue
- clear, self-stick plastic
- plastic sandwich bag
- push pin

### ✳ Prepare
Duplicate the lettering on black paper. Enlarge the stocking pattern to 15" long. Duplicate four stockings on red paper and four fur tops on white paper. Duplicate sixteen candy canes on white paper.

### ✳ Create
**1.** Cover the board with white paper. Use a rectan-gular sponge dipped into a shallow dish of red paint to create a brick pattern on the paper.

**2.** Cut out and attach the lettering to the board. Write the Bible verse at the bottom of the board.

**3.** Cut and fold strips of green paper according to the instant border directions on page 10. Trace the holly leaf border on the folded paper and cut out. Post the border around the board's edges.

**4.** Cut out the stockings and tops. Write one of the following on each: Moses, Elijah, Elisha, Jesus.

**5.** Glue the tops to the stockings. Cover the stock-ings with clear, self-stick plastic and attach them to the board, leaving the area open between the tops and the board.

**6.** Cut out the candy canes. Make red stripes on them. Then write the questions from p. 41 on the fronts and the answers on the backs.

**7.** Cover the canes with clear plastic and store them in a sandwich bag pinned to the bulletin board.

**8.** Invite the students to learn more about biblical miracle-workers by placing the correct candy cane in the right stocking.

### ✳ Teach
Create a game from the board by giving each child a candy cane from which to read. Provide real candy canes for those who guess the correct answers.

Suggested Usage: Christmas

# Questions and Answers for "Miracle Workers"

1. Who turned a rod into a serpent?
2. Who changed Egyptian water into blood?
3. Who parted the Red Sea?
4. Who brought forth water from a stone?
5. Who prayed, and it didn't rain for three-and-a-half years?
6. Who prayed for fire to come down from heaven?
7. Who was taken to heaven in a whirlwind?
8. Who was fed by ravens?
9. Who parted the waters of the Jordan River?
10. Who healed Naaman of leprosy?
11. Who made an ax head float?
12. Who prayed for the Syrian army to be struck blind?
13. Who calmed the raging winds and seas?
14. Who fed 5,000 with five loaves of bread and two fish?
15. Who turned water into wine?
16. Who was resurrected from the dead?

## Answers

| | |
|---|---|
| 1. Moses | 9. Elisha |
| 2. Moses | 10. Elisha |
| 3. Moses | 11. Elisha |
| 4. Moses | 12. Elisha |
| 5. Elijah | 13. Jesus |
| 6. Elijah | 14. Jesus |
| 7. Elijah | 15. Jesus |
| 8. Elijah | 16. Jesus |

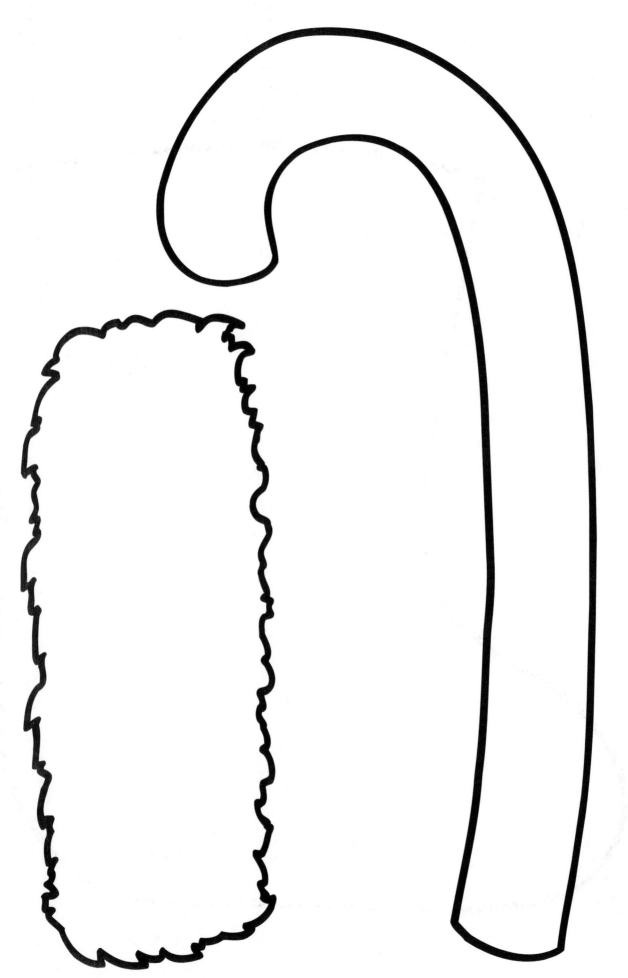

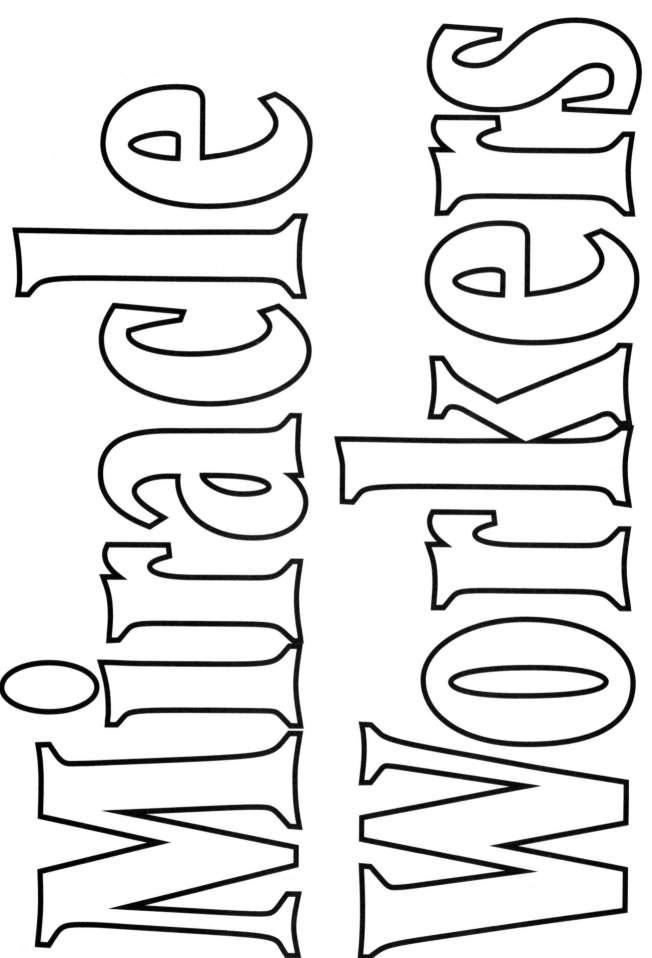

# MYSTERY VERSE

## ✳ Plan

To learn an important Bible verse.

## ✳ Memorize

*For God so loved the world that he gave his one and only Son, that whoever believes in him shall not perish but have eternal life.* John 3:16

## ✳ Gather

- pattern for lettering from p. 48
- pattern for star and ornaments from pp. 46-47
- pattern for tree border from p. 13
- background paper, black
- foil gift wrap
- poster paper, green
- construction paper, green
- Velcro
- crayons
- safety scissors
- push pin
- clear, self-stick plastic
- marker, black
- plastic sandwich bag

## ✳ Prepare

Trace the lettering onto gift wrap. Cut a Christmas tree from green paper (see illustration on p. 46). Trace and cut the star from yellow paper, and duplicate 27 ornaments on white paper.

## ✳ Create

1. Cover the board with black paper. Cut out the lettering and attach it to the board as shown.
2. Cut and fold strips of green paper according to the instant border directions on page 10. Trace the tree border onto the folded paper and cut out. Attach the border around the board's edges.
3. Attach the tree to the bulletin board. Cut out the star and attach it to the top of the tree.
4. Have the children color and cut out the ornaments.
5. Write one word from the memory verse on each ornament. Cover the ornaments with clear, self-stick plastic. Attach Velcro to the backs and to the tree. Place the ornaments in a plastic bag pinned to the board.
6. Have the students arrange the ornaments in order.

## ✳ Teach

Two other ways to use this bulletin board: 1. Have the students color several ornaments each, then change the mystery verse from week to week throughout the Christmas season. 2. Instead of a mystery verse, have the students color and cut out ornaments and write their first names on each ornament. Select an appropriate Christmas verse for the students to memorize. When they recite the verse correctly, attach their ornament to the tree.

Suggested Usage: Christmas

**To make a Christmas tree:**
1. Fold a large piece of paper or poster paper in half.
2. Draw half of a tree on the fold of the paper, as shown.
3. Cut along your drawn lines, but do not cut on the fold.
4. Open up your tree!

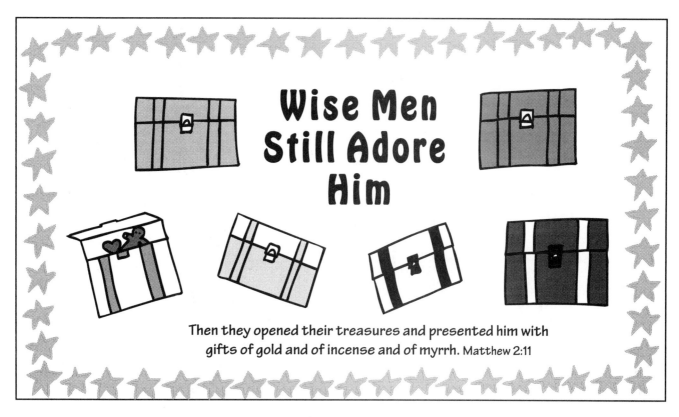

**Then they opened their treasures and presented him with gifts of gold and of incense and of myrrh. Matthew 2:11**

## ✳ Ages 6-10 ✳

### ✳ Plan
To understand that God gave the gift of baby Jesus.

### ✳ Memorize
*Then they opened their treasures and presented him with gifts of gold and of incense and of myrrh.*
Matthew 2:11

### ✳ Gather
• pattern for lettering from p. 53
• pattern for chest from pp. 51-52
• pattern for star border from p. 13
• poster paper, black
• paper, white
• construction paper, yellow, or foil, gold
• chalk
• pencil
• safety scissors

### ✳ Prepare
Duplicate the lettering on yellow paper or gold foil. Duplicate one top and one bottom set for each child on white paper.

### ✳ Create
1. Cover the bulletin board with black background paper. Cut out the lettering and attach it to the board as shown. Write the memory verse with chalk at the bottom of the board.

2. Cut and fold strips of yellow construction paper according to the instant border directions on page 10. Trace the star border pattern onto the folded paper, cut out and unfold. Attach the border around the board's edges.

3. Have the students color and cut out the chest. Show how to glue the top and bottom together (see the illustration on p. 50) and fold the top part of the chest closed, then open again. Ask the children to think about what they would have given baby Jesus and to draw that gift inside the lid of the chest.

4. Fold the lids back over the chests and attach them to the bulletin board.

### ✳ Teach
This project is a good opener for a discussion of gift-giving. Many children do not know that the Christmas tradition of gifts is an act that symbolizes the gift God gave us when he sent baby Jesus. Discuss this concept with the class, then present each child with a small gift to take home as a reminder.

Suggested Usage: Christmas

# How to Make the Treasure Chest

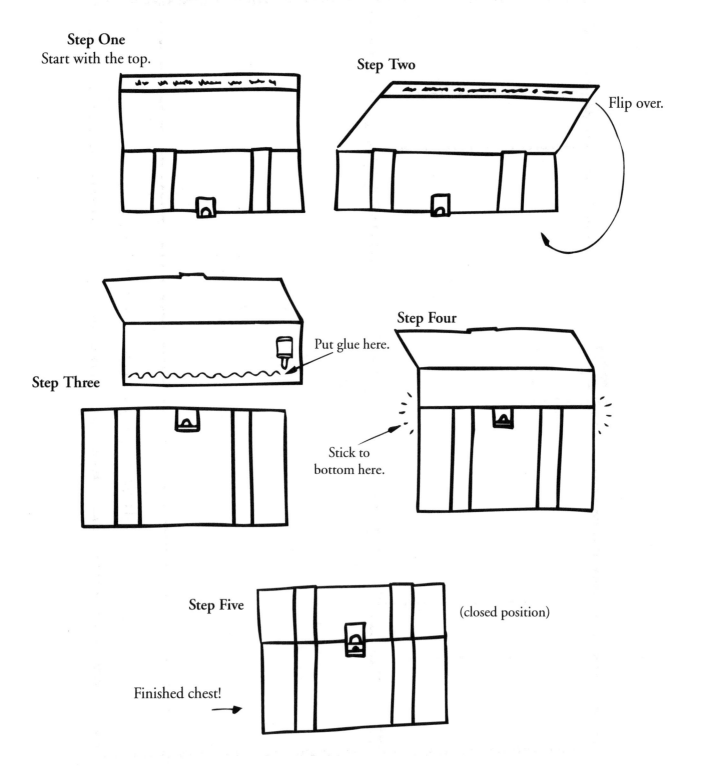

**Step One**
Start with the top.

**Step Two**

Flip over.

**Step Three**

Put glue here.

**Step Four**

Stick to bottom here.

**Step Five**

(closed position)

Finished chest!

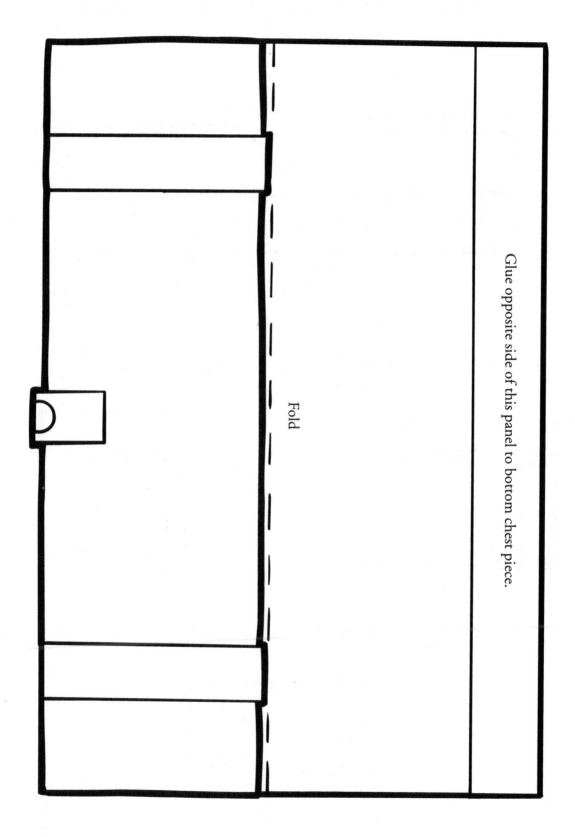

Fold

Glue opposite side of this panel to bottom chest piece.

Wise Men
Adore
Still
Him

## ❋ Plan

To celebrate the joy in following Jesus.

## ❋ Memorize

*He who has the Son has life.* 1 John 5:12

## ❋ Gather

- pattern for party hat from p. 55
- pattern for lettering from pp. 56-57
- pattern for star border from p. 13
- background paper, white or yellow
- construction paper, various colors
- fabric paint pens, various colors
- fabric scraps, ribbon, rick-rack, lace, etc.
- tape
- glue sticks
- elastic (optional)
- stapler
- hole punch (optional)

## ❋ Prepare

Duplicate the lettering and party hat patterns on colored paper. Cut out one hat for each child.

## ❋ Create

1. Attach the background paper to the board. Cut out the lettering and post it on the board.
2. Cut and fold strips of paper according to the instant border directions on page 10. Trace the star border onto the folded paper and cut out.

Staple the border around the edges of the board.
3. Distribute the party hats and have the children decorate them using glue sticks and craft items.
4. Write the students' names on their hats using a fabric paint pen. Shape the hat into a cone and staple it at the seam. Cover the staples with tape. Attach the hats to the board.
5. Cut confetti (shapes large enough for writing) from scrap pieces of paper. Each week, ask the children to name some things that they like about church or a Bible story and write them on the confetti. Staple the confetti to the bulletin board.

## ❋ Teach

You may allow the children to wear the party hats before you attach them to the bulletin board. To make the hats wearable, punch a hole on each side of the hat along the bottom. Cut a piece of elastic long enough to go under the child's chin, place each end of the elastic through the hole, and tie securely. Be sure to cover the hat's staples with tape to avoid scratching. To add to your festive theme, have a "celebrate Jesus" party with cake, punch and noiseblowers to praise Jesus. Sing upbeat church songs that the children enjoy. Repeat the memory verse with the class and emphasize the joy we have as Christians because we have new life.

Suggested Usage: New Year's

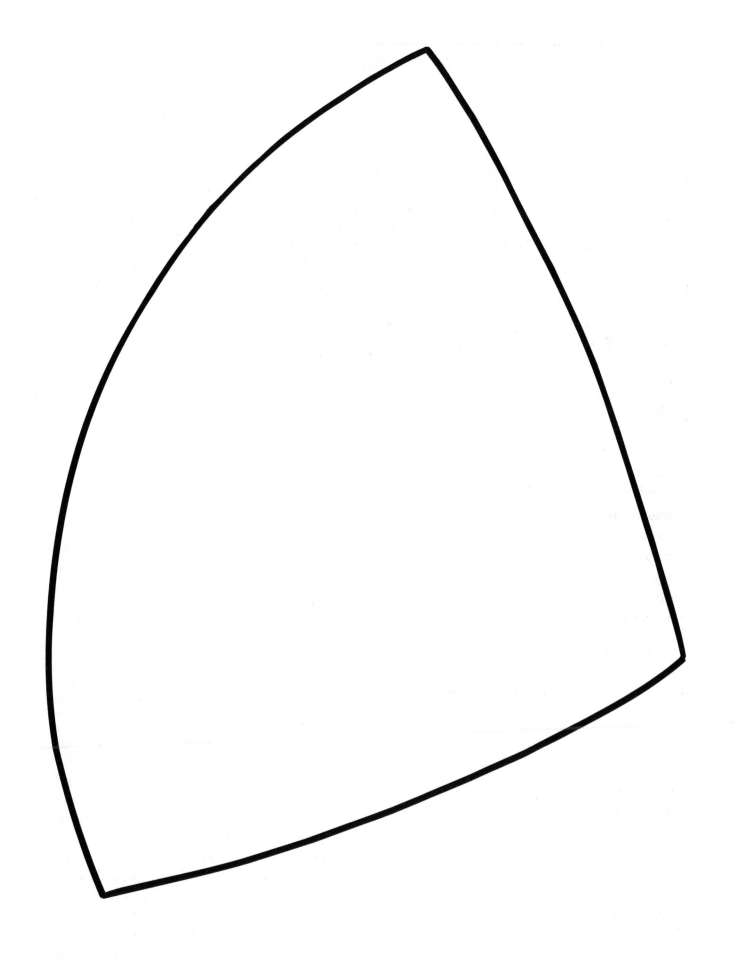

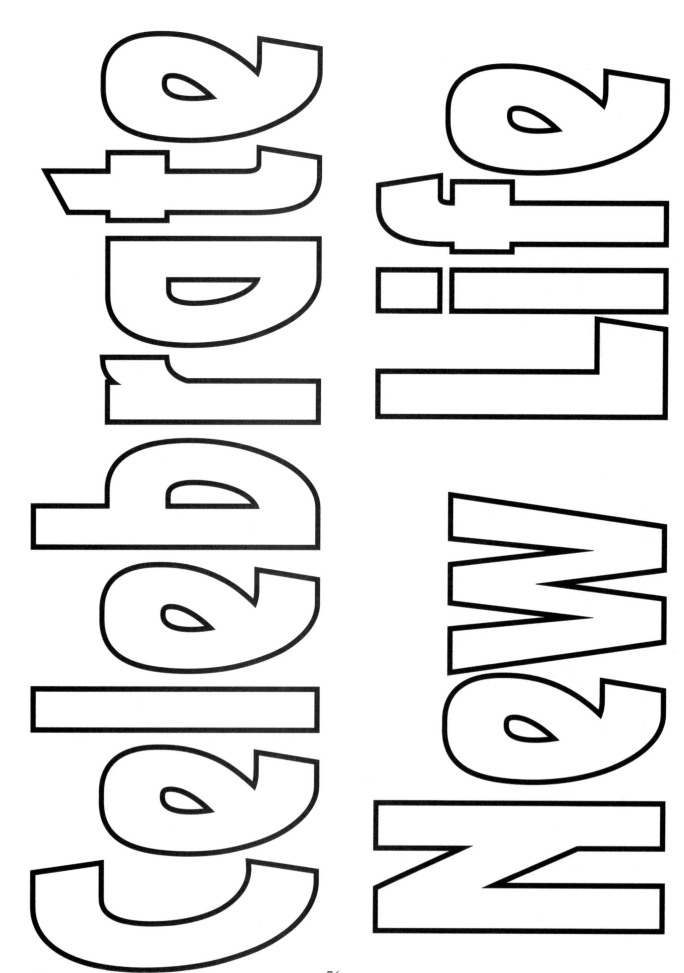

Celebrate Life

New Life

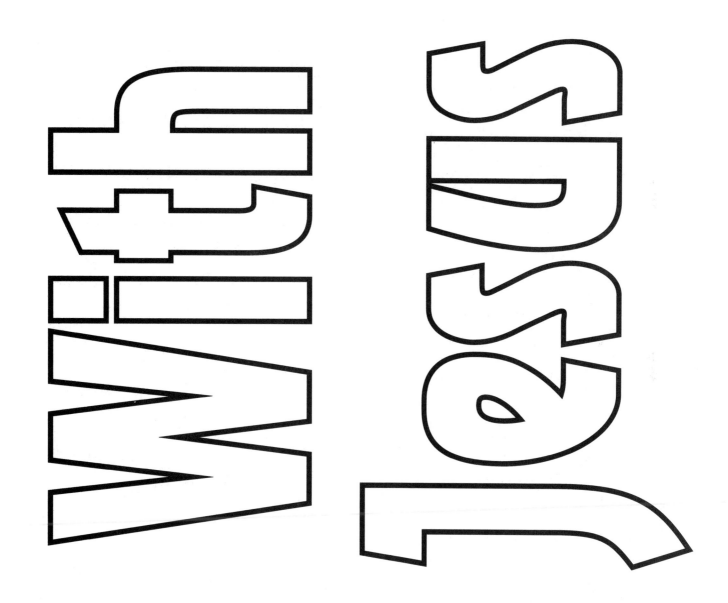

## * Plan

To teach that we must live for Jesus until He returns.

## * Memorize

*Keep watch, because you do not know on what day your Lord will come.* Matthew 24:42

## * Gather

- pattern for clock hands from p. 59
- pattern for lettering from p. 60
- pattern for star border from p. 13
- background paper, any color
- construction paper, black
- marker, black
- hole punch
- paper plates
- crayons
- paper fasteners

## * Prepare

Trace or duplicate one set of clock hands per child on black paper. Duplicate the lettering on a color of paper that coordinates with your background paper.

## * Create

1. Attach the background paper to the board. Cut out the lettering and attach it to the board.
2. Cut and fold strips of paper according to the instant border directions on page 10. Trace the star border onto the folded paper and cut out.

Staple the border around the board's edges.
3. Cut out the clock hands. Punch a hole in each one, hold them together and push a paper fastener through the holes.
4. Write the numbers around the sides of the plates. Distribute them to the children and allow them to color their clocks. Write their names on them.
5. Position the clock hands with the paper fastener in the center of the plate. Push the fastener through the plate and loosely bend the prongs back. Leave the hands to move freely. Allow the children to set their clocks at the time of their choice, then attach the clocks to the board.

## * Teach

Say, **What does it mean when we say, "Happy New Year"? Some year, Jesus will return to take everyone who loves Him to heaven with Him. Should we love Jesus this year? Let's hang our clocks on the bulletin board to remind us that we should love Jesus and keep watch for Him just like our Bible verse says, since we don't know when He might return.** The students may take their clocks home when you dismantle the bulletin board. Write the memory verse on the clocks, and cover the paper fastener prongs with tape.

Suggested Usage: New Year's

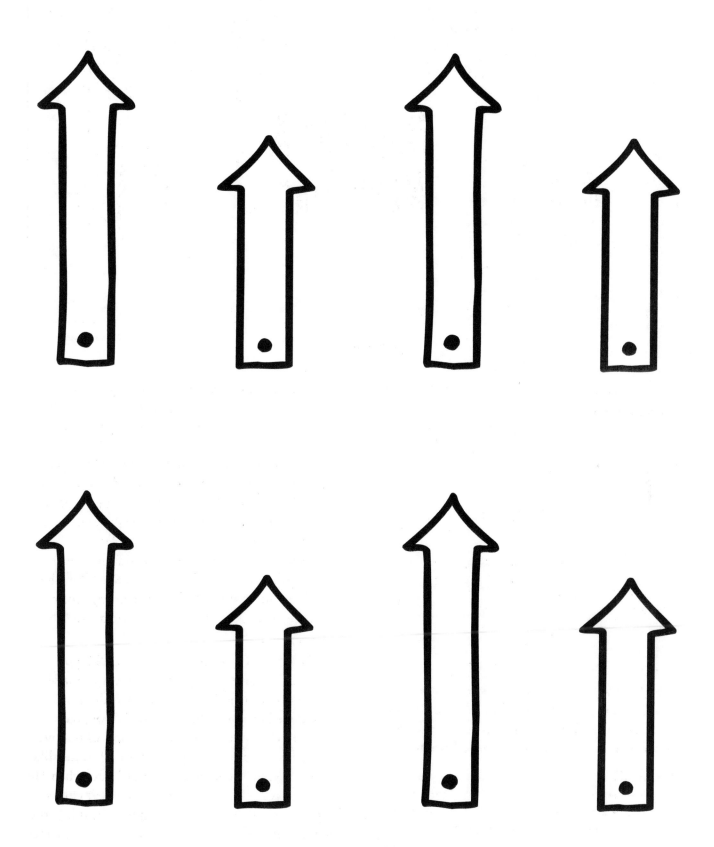

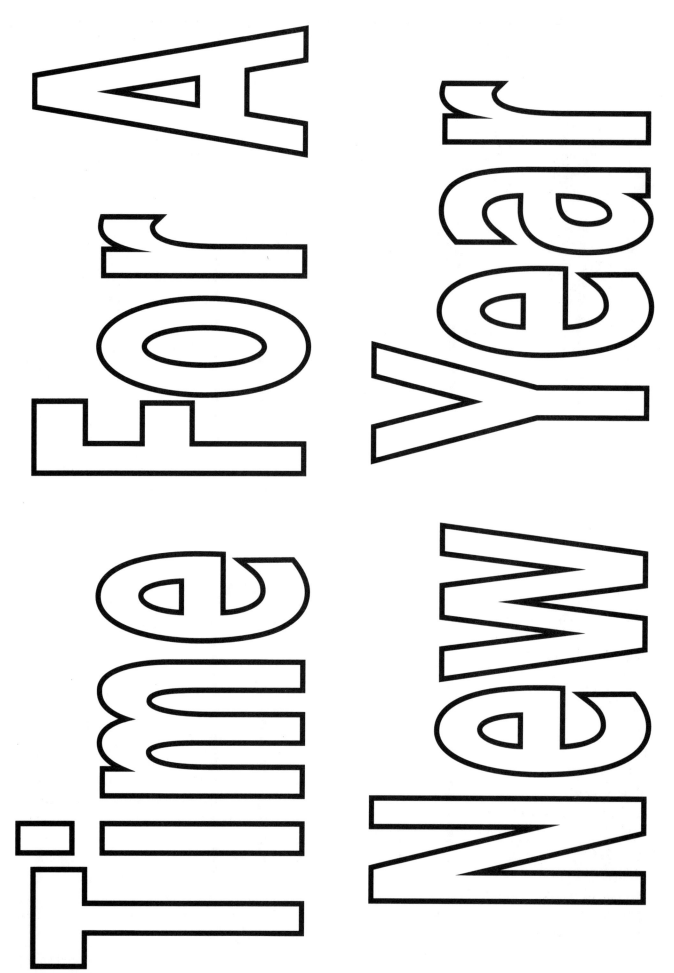

"My great concern is to be on God's side."

— Abraham Lincoln

## ✳ Ages 6-10 ✳

### ✳ Plan
To help children respect Abraham Lincoln as a Christian.

### ✳ Memorize
*The fear of the Lord teaches a man wisdom.*
Proverbs 15:33

### ✳ Gather
• pattern for lettering from p. 64
• pattern for log border from p. 12
• pattern for head and hat from pp. 62-63
• background paper, blue
• construction paper, red, brown and black
• paper, white
• scissors
• glue
• pencils
• marker, black

### ✳ Prepare
Duplicate the lettering on red construction paper. Duplicate the pattern for Lincoln's head and hat on white paper.

### ✳ Create
1. Cover the bulletin board with blue background paper. Cut out and attach the lettering to the board as shown. Use a black marker to write Lincoln's quote at the bottom of the board.
2. Cut and fold strips of brown construction paper according to the directions on page 10. Trace the log border onto the folded paper and cut out. Attach the border around the board's perimeter.
3. Distribute copies of Lincoln's head and hat with black construction paper. Have the students trace and cut out the hat from black construction paper, then color in Lincoln's face.
4. Show how to cut and curl black paper strips (using the side of a pencil) and glue them to Lincoln's face for his beard. Have the class glue the hat to the top of the Lincoln head.
5. Attach the figures to the bulletin board.

### ✳ Teach
Read the quote from Abraham Lincoln, than ask, **Why is it important that Abraham Lincoln chose to be on God's side? Lincoln is considered by many people to have been one of this country's greatest presidents. Is it just as important for us to be on God's side like Lincoln said he was? Why?** You may allow the children to take home their Lincoln figures when you dismantle the bulletin board. Have them copy the quote from Lincoln and the Bible verse on the back of the head before leaving class.

Suggested Usage: Presidents' Day

Abraham

Lincoln

### ✳ Plan

To know that God loves us more than we love Him.

### ✳ Memorize

*Love the Lord your God with all your heart.*
Matthew 22:37

### ✳ Gather

- pattern for heart border from p. 11
- pattern for lettering from p. 68
- patterns for heart and cross from pp. 66-67
- background paper, white
- construction paper, red and white
- glue
- Velcro
- straight pins or push pins

### ✳ Prepare

Duplicate the lettering on red construction paper.

### ✳ Create

1. Post white background paper on the bulletin board. Cut out the lettering and attach it to the board as shown in the illustration.
2. Cut and fold strips of red construction paper according to the instant border directions on page 10. Trace the heart border pattern onto the folded paper and cut out the border. Staple the border around the edges of the board.
3. Trace and cut out a large heart from red construction or poster paper as shown in the illustration on p. 67.
4. Make the cross by tracing and cutting it from white construction paper. Enlarge or reduce it as desired. Glue it in the center of the heart.
5. Cut the heart into several pieces. Put it together correctly and temporarily pin it to the bulletin board. (Store the pins away before the children arrive.) Place Velcro on corresponding heart pieces and their places on the bulletin board.

### ✳ Teach

After the children have had opportunities to play with the puzzle, ask, **What does a heart mean? What does a cross mean? Does this mean that we should love God? How can we show God we love Him?** Lead the class in a short prayer before closing, such as, **God, thank You for loving us. Our lives are not a puzzle as long as we follow You. We love You with all of our hearts. Amen.**

Suggested Usage: Valentine's Day

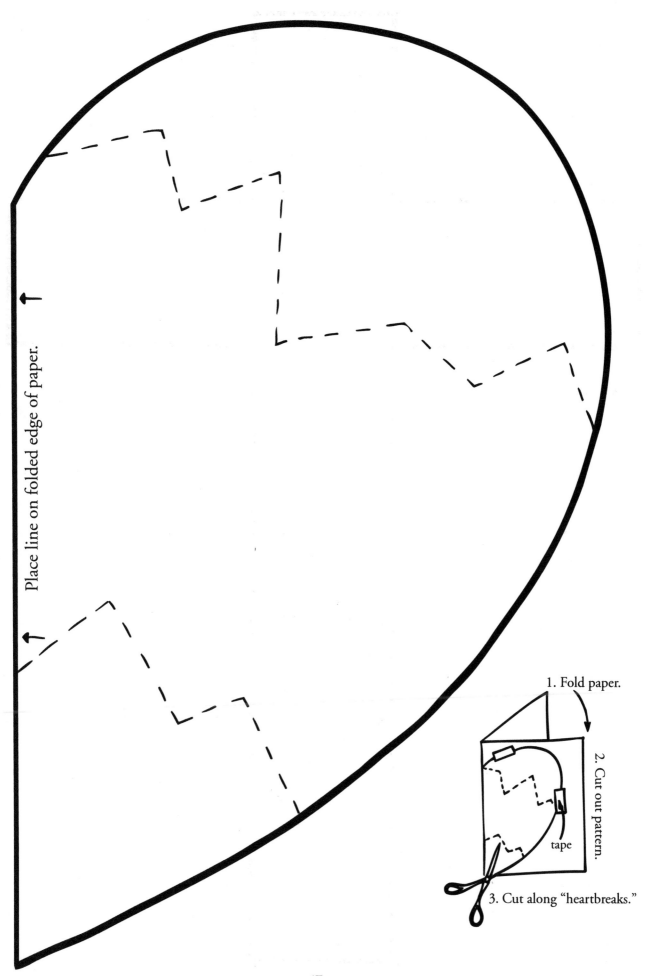

Place line on folded edge of paper.

1. Fold paper.

2. Cut out pattern.

tape

3. Cut along "heartbreaks."

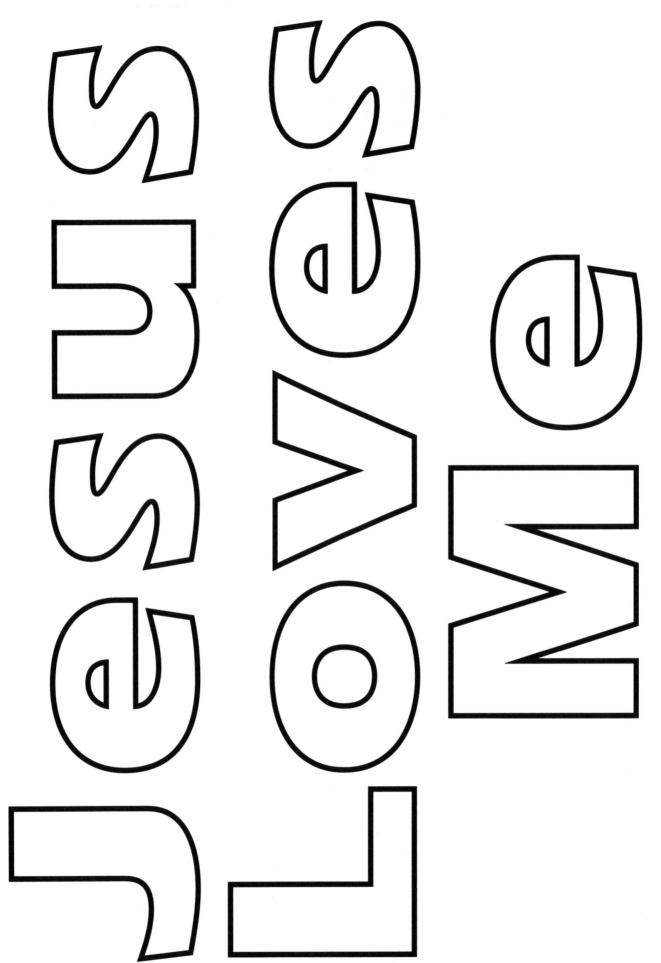

Jesus Loves Me

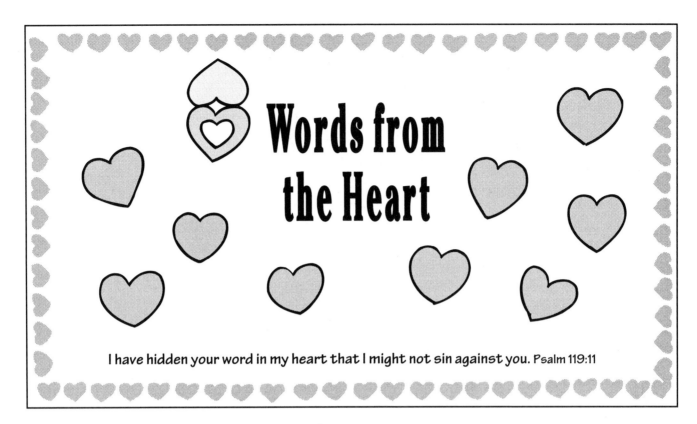

**Words from the Heart**

I have hidden your word in my heart that I might not sin against you. Psalm 119:11

❋ **Ages 6-10** ❋

❋ **Plan**
To learn Bible verses related to love.

❋ **Memorize**
*I have hidden your word in my heart that I might not sin against you.* Psalm 119:11

❋ **Gather**
• pattern for lettering from p. 71
• patterns for hearts from p. 70
• pattern for heart border from p. 11
• background paper, pastel-colored
• construction paper, black and red
• marker, black
• safety scissors
• glue
• Bibles
• Bible concordances
• pens or markers
• small candy hearts

❋ **Prepare**
Duplicate the lettering on black paper, and the large and small hearts on white paper, one set per student.

❋ **Create**
1. Cover the board with pastel-colored background paper. Cut out the lettering and attach it to the board. Write the Bible verse on the bottom.

2. Cut and fold strips of red paper according to the instant border directions on page 10. Trace the heart border pattern onto the folded paper and cut out. Attach it around the board's edges.

3. Distribute the duplicated heart patterns. Have the students trace the large heart onto a piece of folded red construction paper. Show how to cut it out and unfold it. Have them trace the smaller heart on white paper (not folded). Show how to glue the white heart inside the red one.

4. Help the students use Bibles and concordances to find scripture verses related to love. Instruct them to write their names on the fronts of the closed hearts and to select a favorite from the love Bible verses and write it on the white heart.

5. Attach the hearts to the bulletin board.

❋ **Teach**
Write the memory verse on a copy of the large heart, then make several copies. Cut each one in two pieces down the center, using jagged cuts. Give each child half, then instruct the class to find their partners. Once two partners find each other, they must repeat the Bible verse together for the teacher. Reward the teams with small candy hearts.

Suggested Usage: Valentine's Day

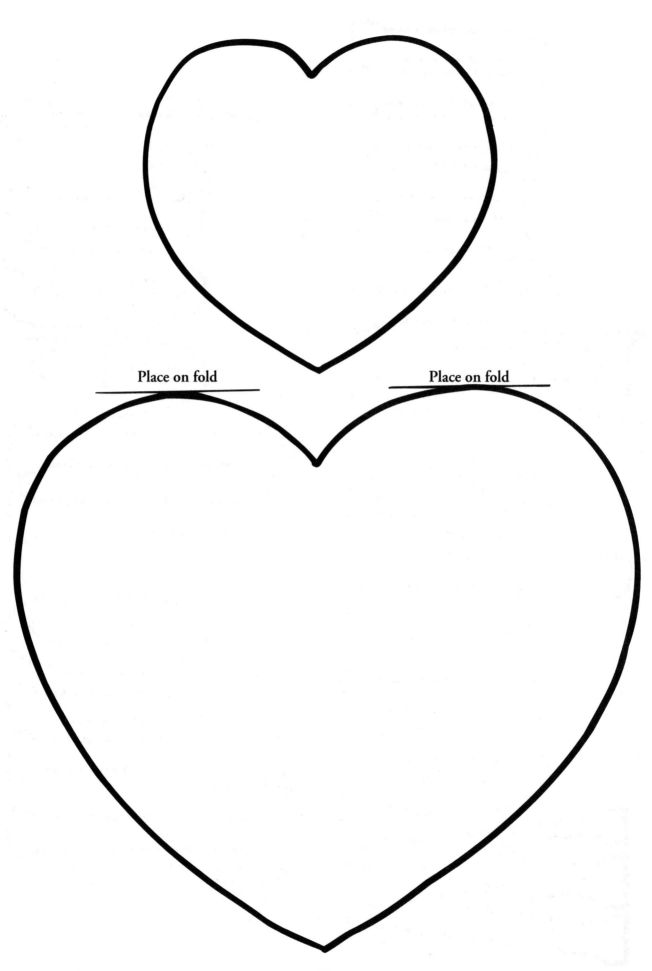

Place on fold          Place on fold

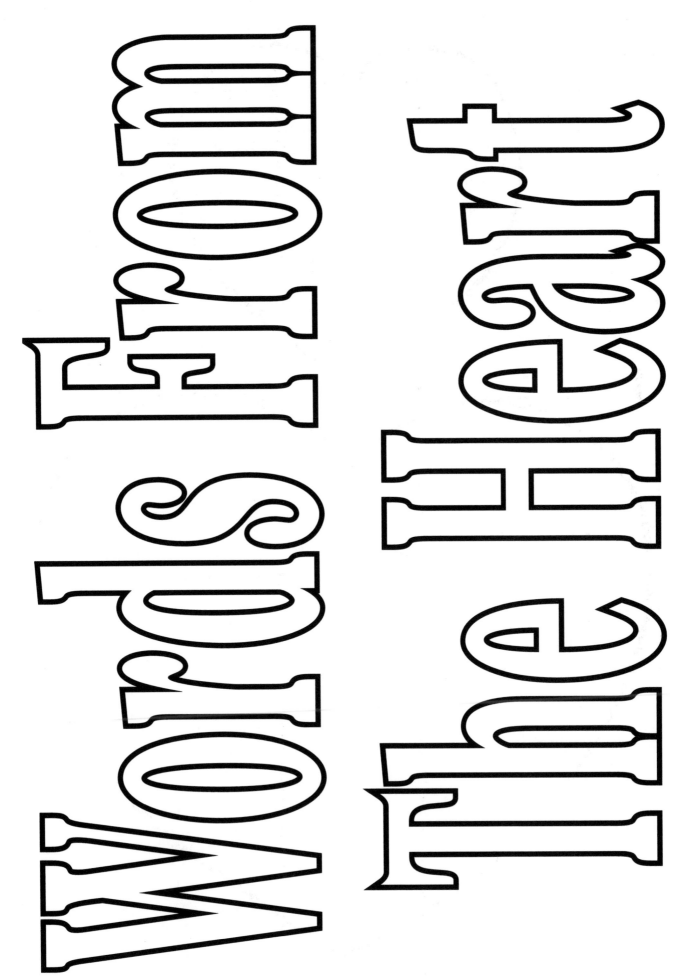

Words From The Heart

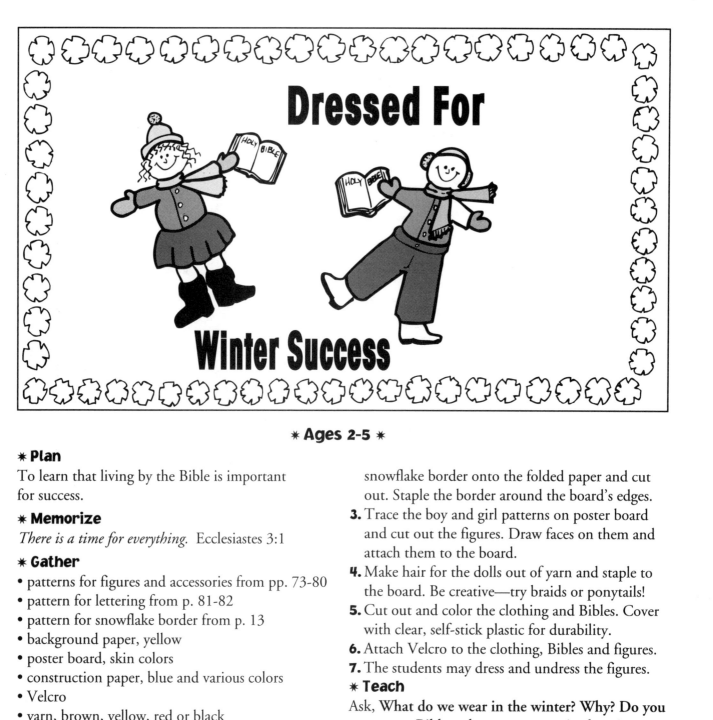

**Dressed For Winter Success**

✳ Ages 2-5 ✳

### ✳ Plan

To learn that living by the Bible is important for success.

### ✳ Memorize

*There is a time for everything.* Ecclesiastes 3:1

### ✳ Gather

- patterns for figures and accessories from pp. 73-80
- pattern for lettering from p. 81-82
- pattern for snowflake border from p. 13
- background paper, yellow
- poster board, skin colors
- construction paper, blue and various colors
- Velcro
- yarn, brown, yellow, red or black
- markers or paint
- clear, self-stick paper
- crayons or watercolors

### ✳ Prepare

Duplicate the lettering on blue paper.

### ✳ Create

1. Attach the yellow paper to the board. Cut out the lettering and post it on the board.
2. Cut and fold strips of paper according to the instant border directions on page 10. Trace the snowflake border onto the folded paper and cut out. Staple the border around the board's edges.
3. Trace the boy and girl patterns on poster board and cut out the figures. Draw faces on them and attach them to the board.
4. Make hair for the dolls out of yarn and staple to the board. Be creative—try braids or ponytails!
5. Cut out and color the clothing and Bibles. Cover with clear, self-stick plastic for durability.
6. Attach Velcro to the clothing, Bibles and figures.
7. The students may dress and undress the figures.

### ✳ Teach

Ask, **What do we wear in the winter? Why? Do you carry your Bible to keep you warm in the winter? Of course not, but we do carry our Bibles so we can look at them to warm our insides and help us learn to love God more. Open your Bible. Say, Let's all gather around the Bible and get warm for a minute while we read about God's love for us. We will always be dressed for success, like the bulletin board says, if we read our Bibles on a regular basis.** Read a Bible story from your Bible or a Bible story book placed inside your Bible. Encourage the children to come close to you and pretend to warm their hands by the "fire" of God's Word.

Suggested Usage: Winter

## How to Make the Boy and Girl Figures

1. Duplicate and cut out the pattern on this page for the top half of the body.
2. Fold a large piece of paper or poster board in half.
3. Lay the pattern on the folded paper as shown below.
4. Trace the pattern onto the large paper.
5. Cut out.
6. Repeat for bottom half of body, using pattern on p. 74. Make two figures.

Lay on fold and cut out.

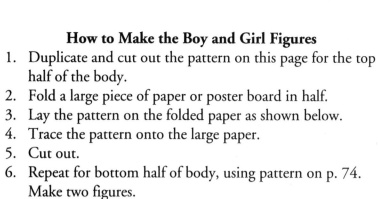

fold

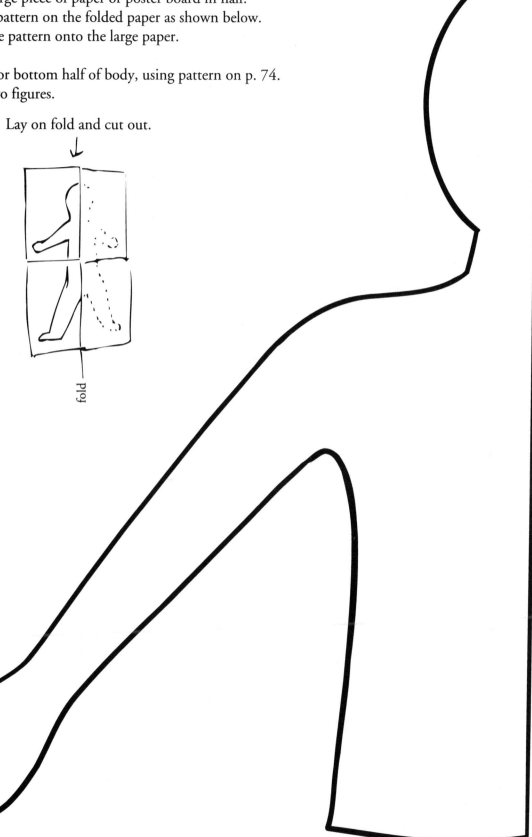

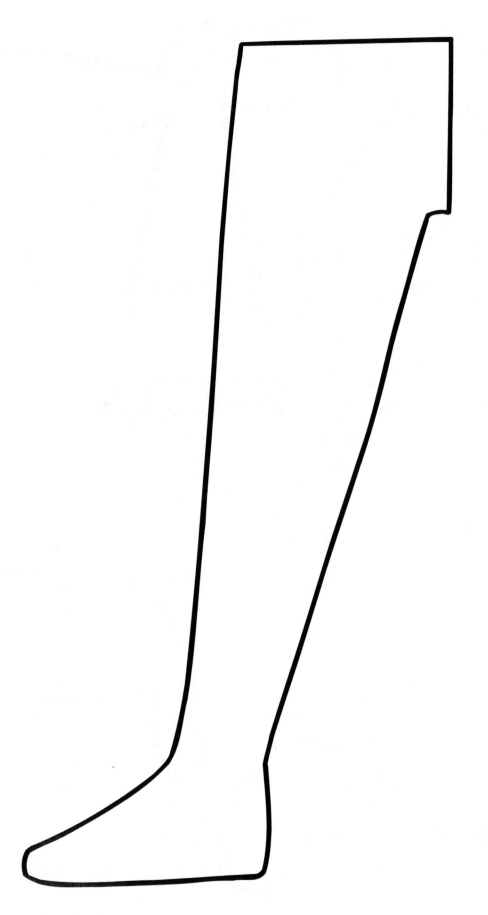

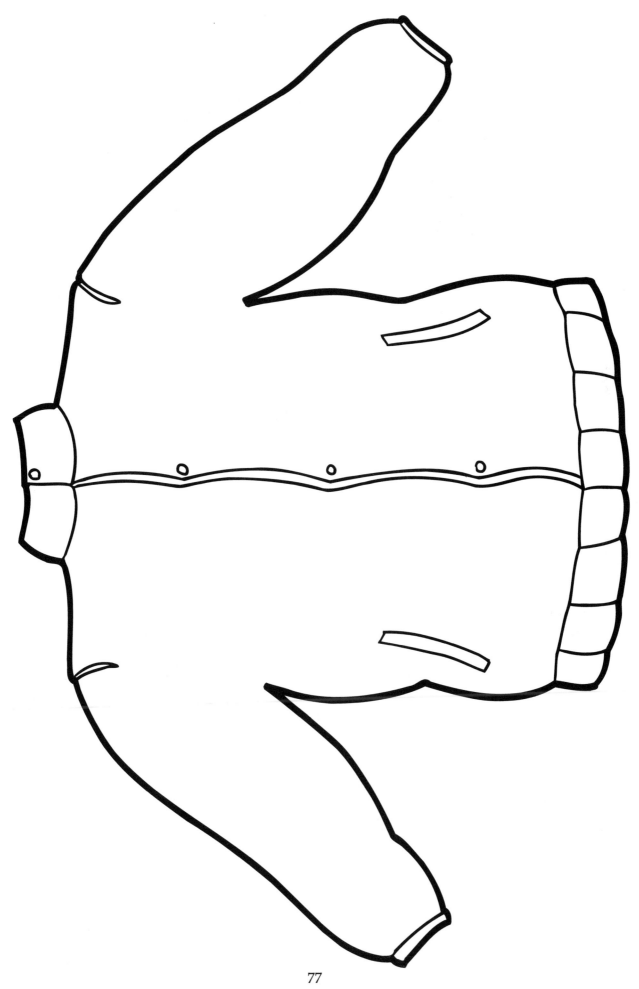

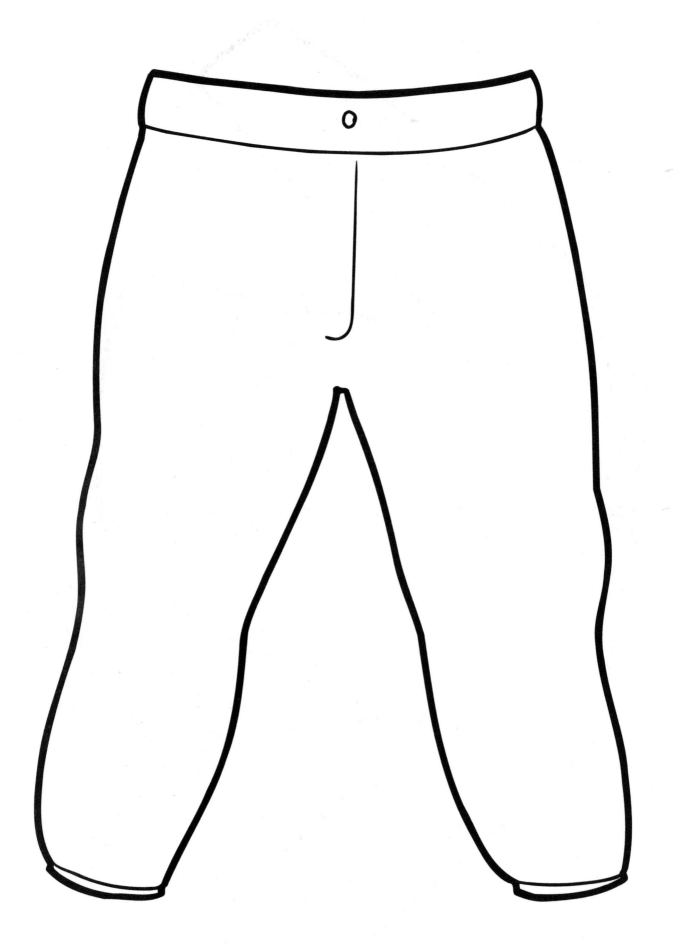

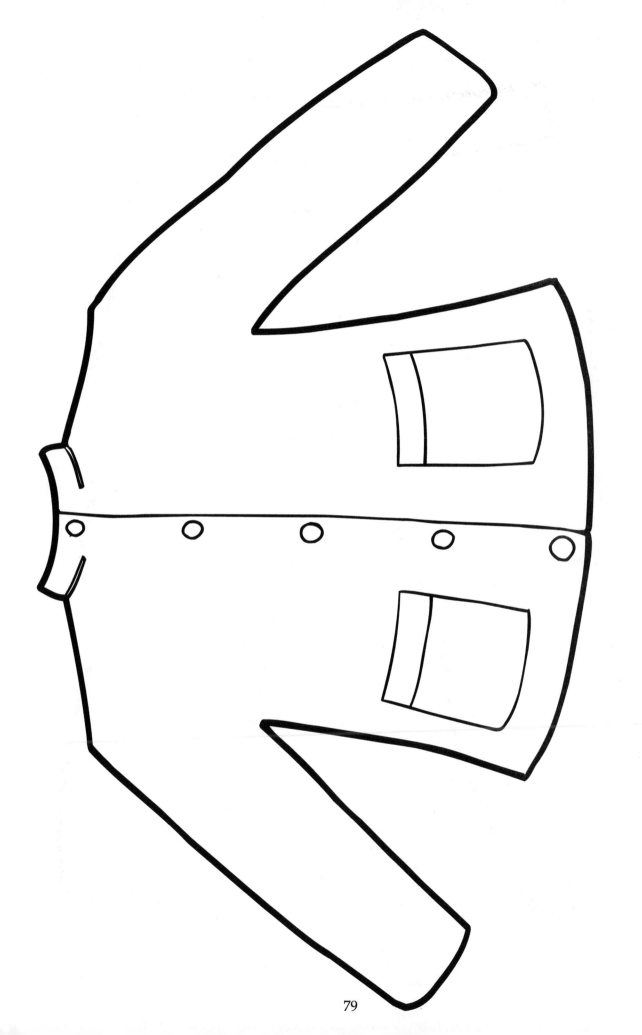

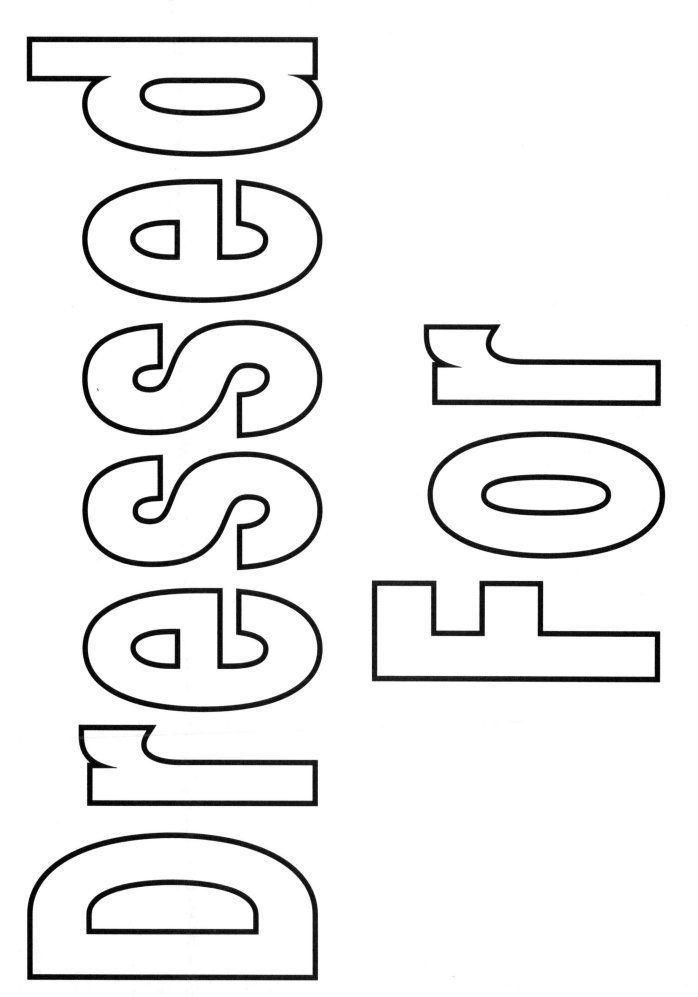

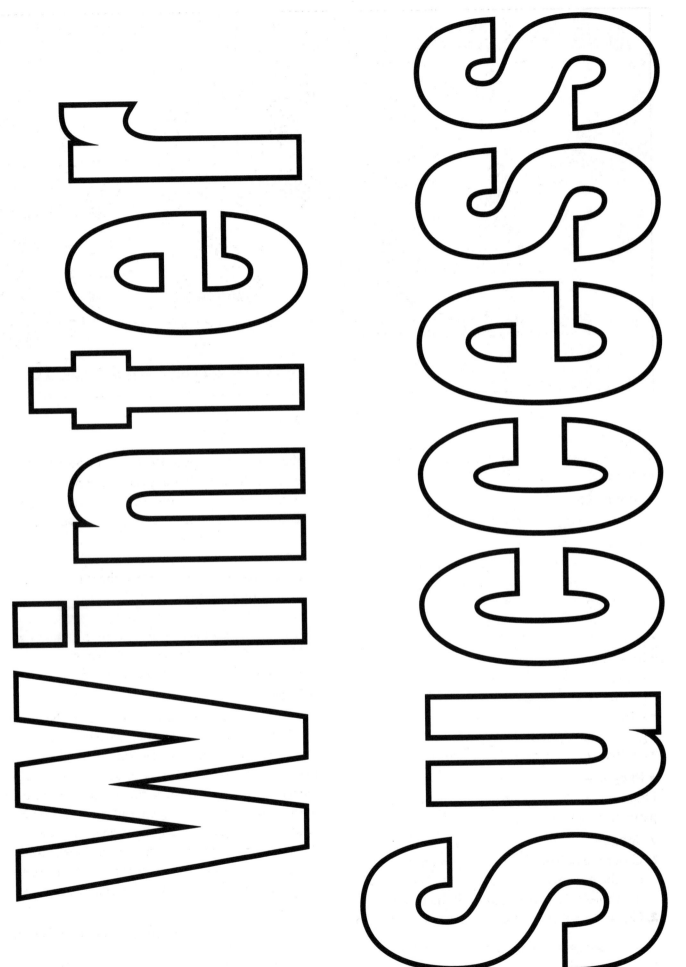

**Bear One Another's Burdens**

Bear one another's burdens.
Galatians 6:2

## ✳ Ages 6-10 ✳

### ✳ Plan
To learn that God intends for us to support each other.

### ✳ Memorize
*Bear one another's burdens.* Galatians 6:2 (KJV)

### ✳ Gather
- pattern for lettering from pp. 86-87
- pattern for bear border from p. 13
- pattern for bear from pp. 84-85
- construction paper, brown, white, pink and black
- paper, white
- background paper, pink
- marker, black
- pencils
- safety scissors
- glue
- construction paper scraps, assorted colors

### ✳ Prepare
Duplicate the lettering on black paper, and the bear patterns on white paper.

### ✳ Create
1. Cover the bulletin board with pink paper. Cut out the lettering and attach it to the board. Write the Bible verse at the bottom of the board.
2. Cut and fold strips of brown paper according to the directions on page 10. Trace the bear border onto the folded paper and cut out the border. Attach the border around the board's perimeter.
3. Distribute one set of bear patterns to each student. Show how to trace and cut the circles from brown, pink, black or white construction paper as directed on the patterns. Have the students use glue to assemble the bear heads.
4. Allow the children to create hats, earmuffs and scarves for their bears from colorful paper scraps. Have them glue the items on the bears.
5. Attach the bears to the bulletin board.

### ✳ Teach
Ask, **What is a burden? Our verse says to "bear one another's burdens." How could we bear each other's burdens?** Split the class into pairs (if you have an uneven number you can partner with the remaining child). Encourage the students to share a burden with each other. Then lead the whole class in prayer, including some quiet time for the students to silently pray for their partners' burdens. After prayer, remind the students to continue to remember to bear each other's burdens during the week ahead.

Suggested Usage: General

nose

outer eyes

face

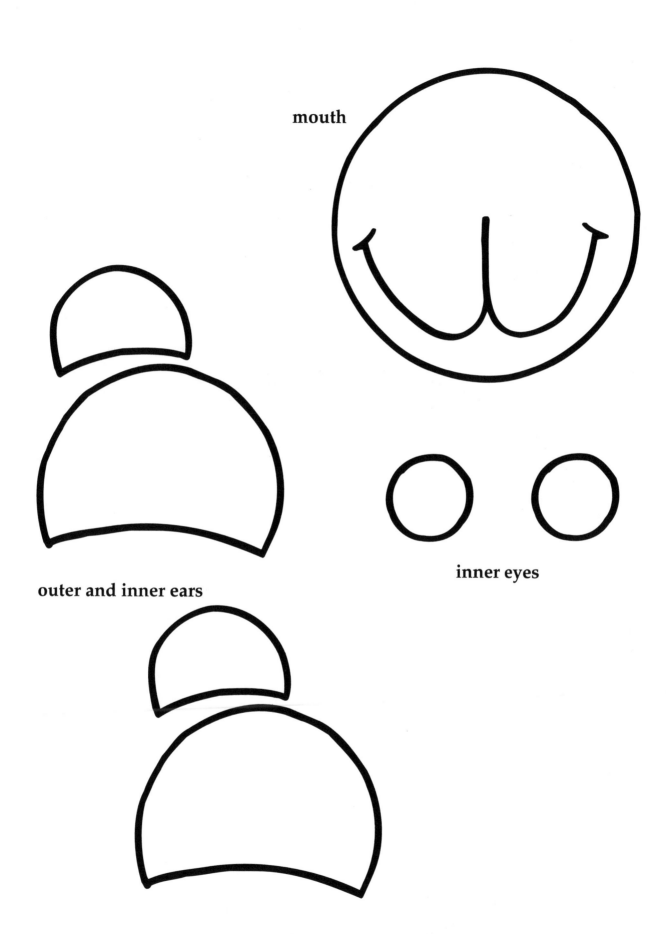

mouth

inner eyes

outer and inner ears

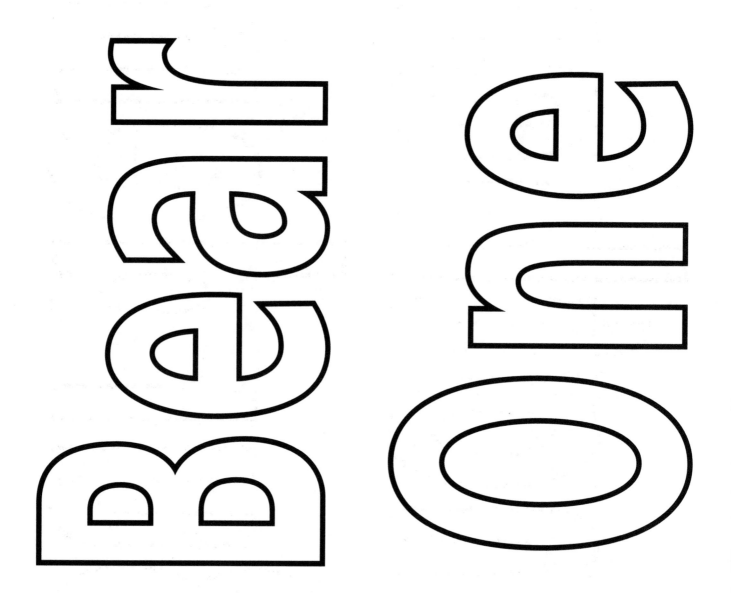

Bear One

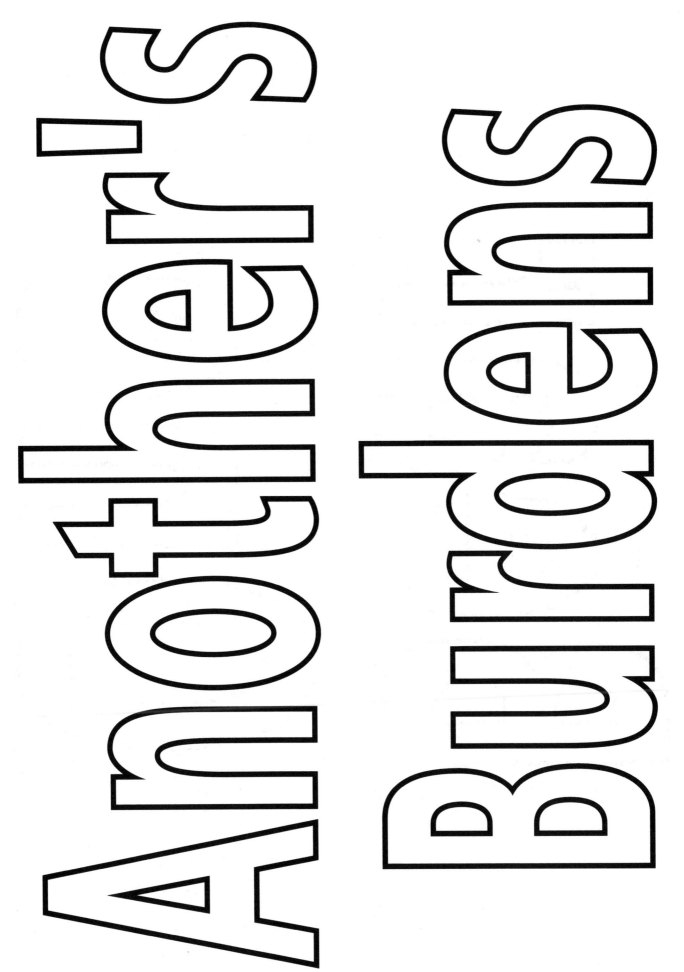

**HOOP IT UP**

I press on toward the goal. Philippians 3:14

## ✳ Plan

To explain the true goal in life.

## ✳ Memorize

*I press on toward the goal.* Philippians 3:14

## ✳ Gather

• patterns for basketballs and boards from pp. 89-91
• pattern for star border from p. 13
• pattern for lettering from p. 92
• background paper, any color
• construction paper, white, orange and black
• marker, black
• nylon net, white

## ✳ Prepare

Duplicate the lettering on a color of construction paper that coordinates with your background paper.

## ✳ Create

1. Attach the background paper to the bulletin board. Cut out and post the lettering at the top of the board. Use the black marker to write the memory verse at the bottom of the board.
2. Cut and fold strips of construction paper according to the instant border directions on page 10. Trace the star border pattern onto the folded paper and cut out the border. Staple the border around the edges of the board.
3. Make two basketball rims by tracing and cutting strips of black construction paper using the patterns on page 90. Bring the ends of one band together in a circle and staple. Glue or staple half of the net material to the inside bottom half of the band so that it resembles a basketball goal. Repeat the process for the second goal.
4. Trace and cut two backboards for the goals from white construction paper. Align the two backboards and attach them to the bulletin board.
5. Staple the basketball hoops to the backboard on the bulletin board.
6. Trace the basketballs on orange construction paper and cut out. Use the black marker to draw the details and to write each child's name on a ball. Attach the balls in various spots on the board as decorations.
7. Wad up scrap paper to make paper "basketballs" for the children to throw.

## ✳ Teach

Use this bulletin board to encourage scripture verse memorization or good behavior by allowing the children to shoot a basket. Keep points and award prizes to those who achieve a designated point level.

Suggested Usage: Basketball season

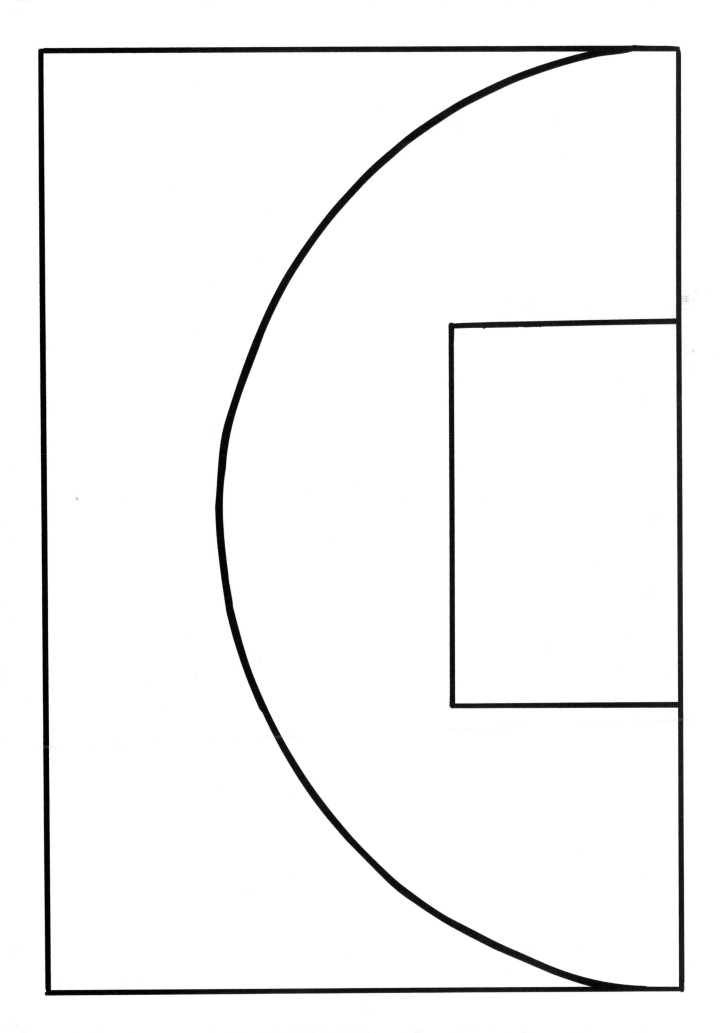

90

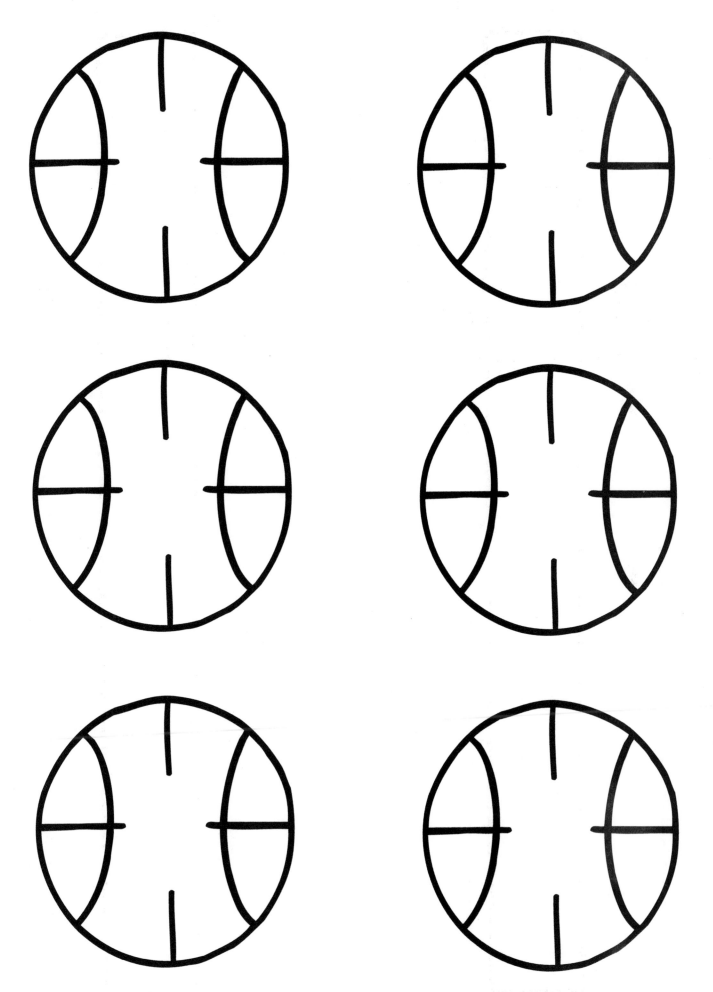

**✳ Ages 2-5 ✳**

## ✳ Plan
To emphasize that God is the Creator of weather.

## ✳ Memorize
*He says to the snow, "Fall on the earth."* Job 37:6

## ✳ Gather
- patterns for snowman and parts from pp. 94-97
- pattern for snowflake border from p. 13
- pattern for lettering from p. 98
- background paper, blue
- construction paper, white, black, brown and orange
- glue
- marker, black
- plastic sandwich bags

## ✳ Prepare
Trace or duplicate the lettering and the snowman on white paper; the arms on brown paper; the eyes, mouth, buttons and hat on black paper; and the nose on orange paper. Cut out one set of snowman parts per child.

## ✳ Create
1. Attach the blue background paper to the board. Cut out and attach the lettering on the board.
2. Cut and fold strips of white paper according to the instant border directions on page 10. Trace the snowflake border on the folded paper and cut out. Staple the border around the board's edges.
3. Cut out the snowmen body pieces. Write each child's name along the bottom of the largest piece on each snowman. Glue the body pieces together so that they slightly overlap. Attach the snowmen to the bulletin board.
4. Cut out the arms, eyes, mouth, buttons, hat and nose. Place each set of pieces in a sandwich bag and attach each bag near a snowman on the bulletin board.
5. Each week the children are present, have them take a piece from their plastic bag and glue it to the snowman. If they attend each week they will create a complete snowman.

## ✳ Teach
When you are finished using this bulletin board, the children may take their snowmen home. Provide glue for the students to secure the arms on their snowmen and to attach any pieces from sessions when they were absent. Write the memory verse on the bottom of their snowmen, repeating it several times as you reiterate that God is the Creator of weather and all that is on the earth.

Suggested Usage: Winter

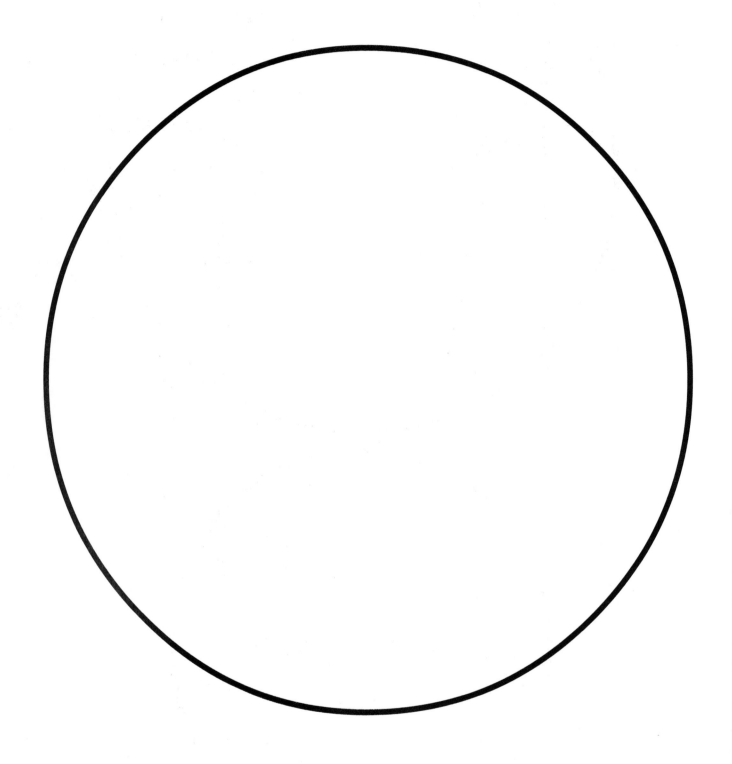

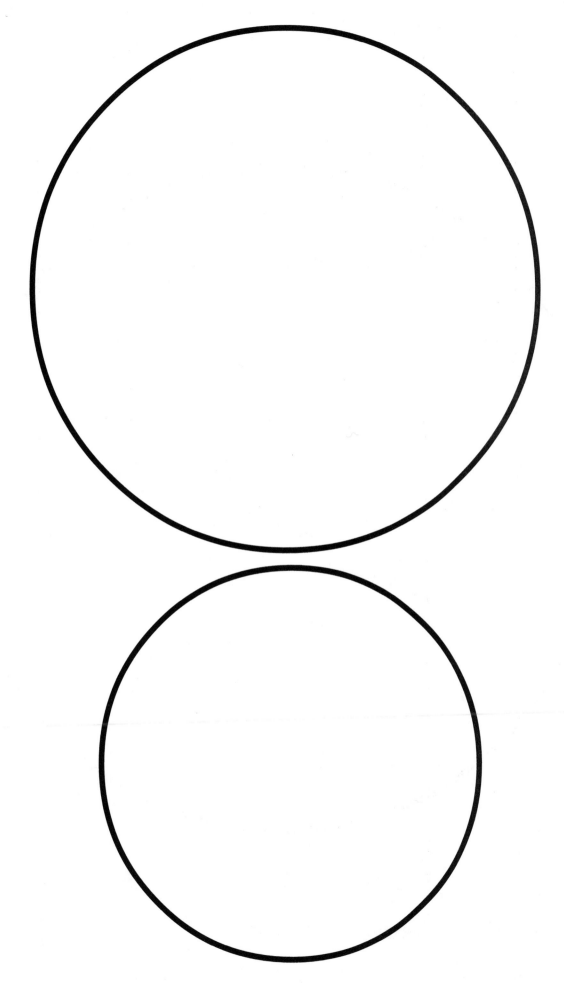

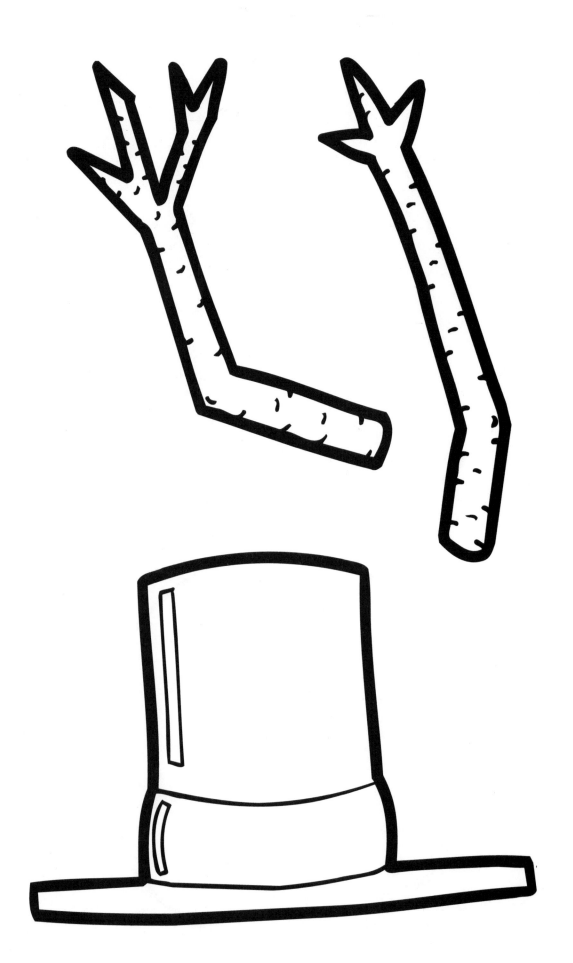

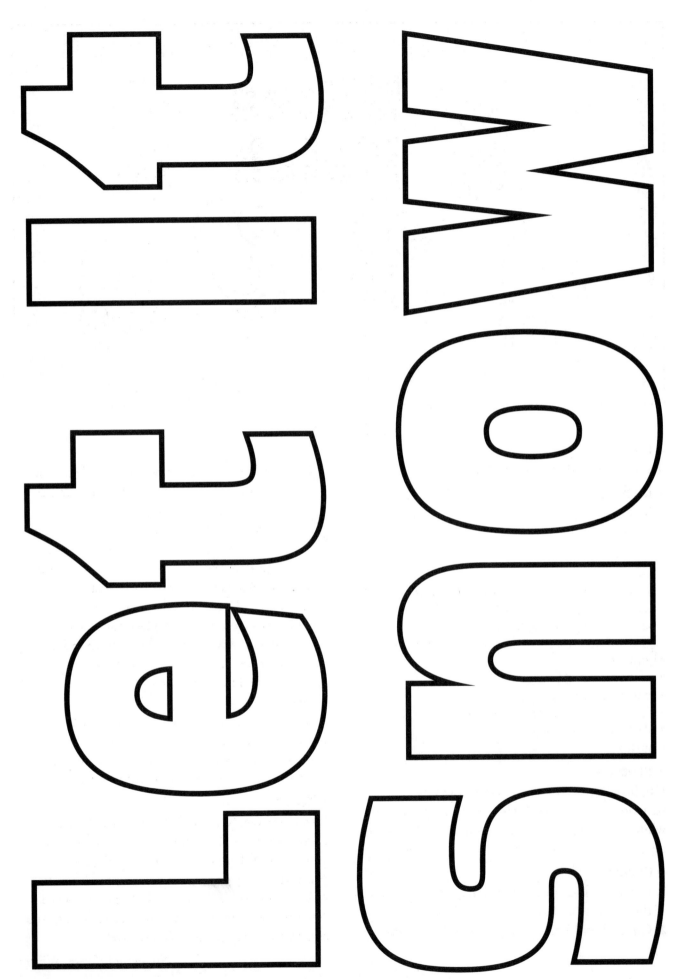

## ✳ Plan

To strengthen Bible verse knowledge.

## ✳ Memorize

*Christ Jesus came into the world to save sinners.*
1 Timothy 1:15

## ✳ Gather

- pattern for lettering from p. 103
- pattern for mitten and snowball from pp. 101-102
- pattern for mitten border from p. 12
- background paper, light blue
- construction paper, white and assorted colors
- crayons
- safety scissors
- marker, black
- clear, self-stick plastic
- plastic sandwich bag
- push pin

## ✳ Prepare

Duplicate the lettering on various colors of construction paper, and the mitten and snowballs on white paper, one set for each student, plus extras for decoration. Cut out the extras.

## ✳ Create

1. Cover the board with light blue paper. Cut out the lettering and attach it to the board.
2. Cut and fold strips of paper according to the instant border directions on page 10. Trace the mitten border on the folded paper and cut out. Post around the board's edges.
3. Distribute the mittens and snowballs. Have the students color and cut out them out. Write one of the Bible verses from page 100 on each mitten, and the reference on a snowball. Write the answers on the backs of the snowballs. Cover them with clear, self-stick plastic and attach them to the board, leaving space between thumb and finger. Store the snowballs in a plastic sandwich bag attached to the right hand corner of the board with a push pin.
4. Write the answers on one extra snowball.
5. Have the students match the snowballs to the correct mittens and place them in the mittens. They may flip over the snowballs for the answers.

## ✳ Teach

Encourage your class to help others by sponsoring a mitten drive: a collection of mittens for the needy. Have the children make posters to hang in the church and neighborhood advertising a drop-off point for the items. Rehearse with the students a "commercial" they may act out or read during your church's worship service. Be creative!

Suggested Usage: Winter

## Scriptures and references for "Mitten Match"

1.  The holy one to be born will be called the Son of God. Luke 1:35

2.  You are the Christ, the Son of the living God. Matthew 16:16

3.  Jesus Christ is the same yesterday and today and forever. Hebrews 13:8

4.  Today in the town of David a Savior has been born to you; he is Christ the Lord. Luke 2:11

5.  She will give birth to a son, and you are to give him the name Jesus, because he will save his people from their sins. Matthew 1:21

6.  Christ Jesus came into the world to save sinners. 1 Timothy 1:15

7.  I am returning to my Father and your Father, to my God and your God. John 20:17

8.  You are all sons of God through faith in Christ Jesus. Galatians 3:26

9.  Nothing is impossible with God. Luke 1:37

10. God created man in his own image, in the image of God he created him; male and female he created them. Genesis 1:27

11. Know that the Lord is God. It is he who made us, and we are his; we are his people, the sheep of his pasture. Psalm 100:3

12. Come, let us bow down in worship, let us kneel before the Lord our maker. Psalm 95:6

13. May the grace of the Lord Jesus Christ, and the love of God, and the fellowship of the Holy Spirit be with you all. 2 Corinthians 13:14

14. The Counselor, the Holy Spirit, whom the Father will send in my name, will teach you all things and will remind you of everything I have said to you. John 14:26

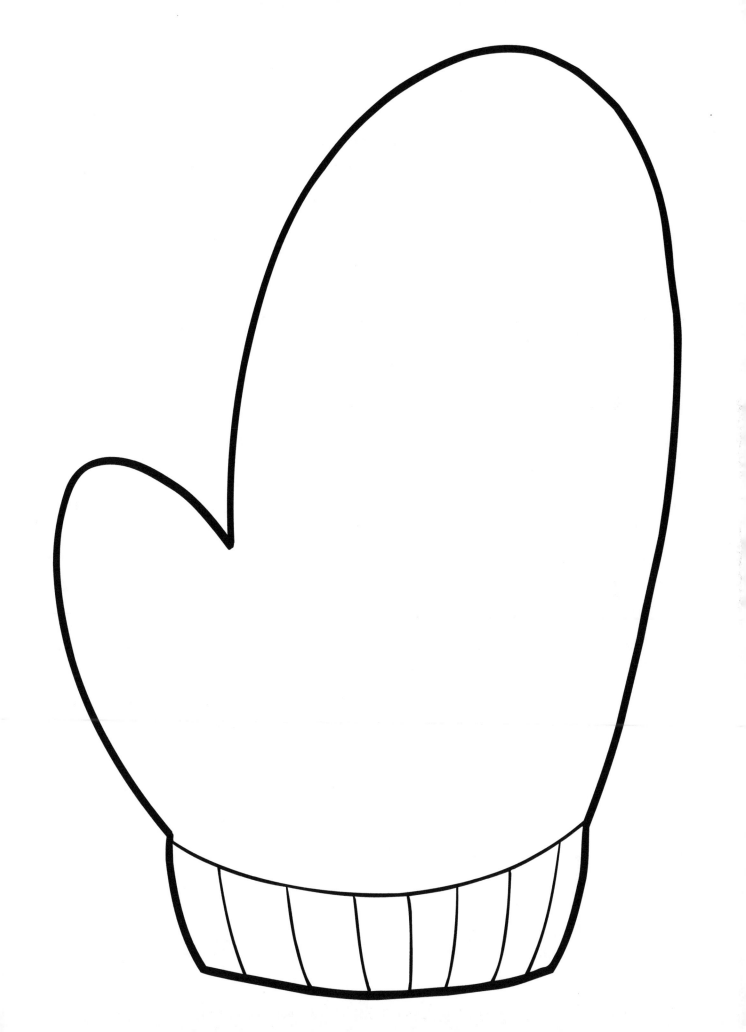

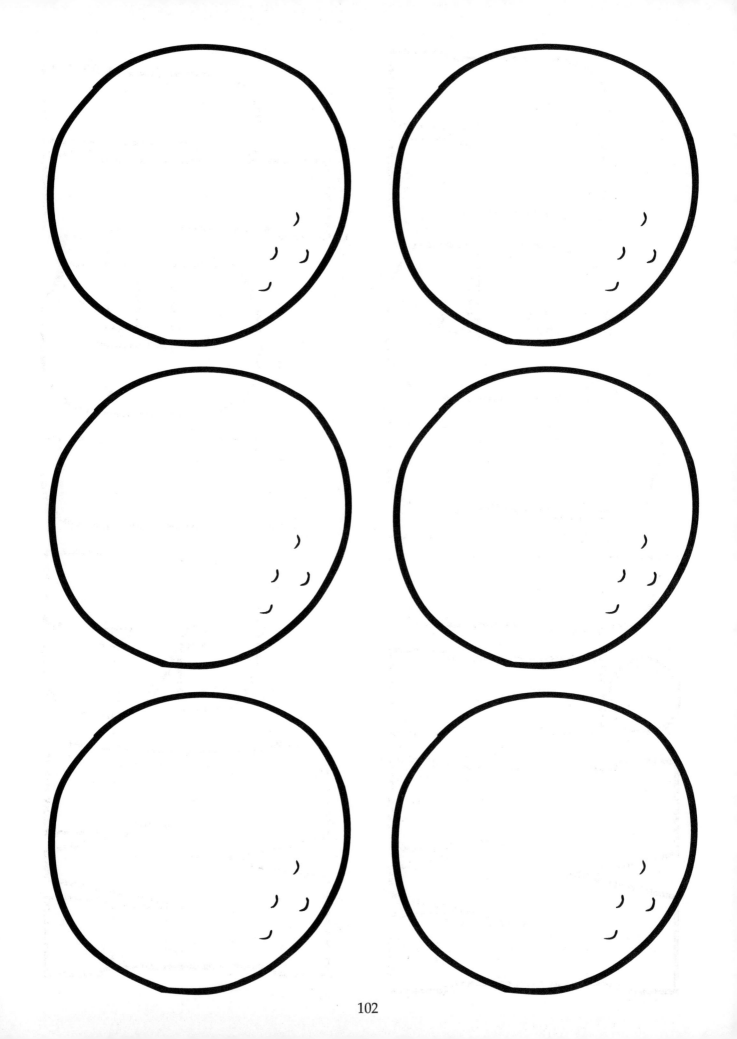

Wash me, and I will be whiter than snow. Psalm 51:7

## ✳ Ages 2-5 ✳

### ✳ Plan
To explain that God makes our lives clean and whole.

### ✳ Memorize
*Wash me, and I will be whiter than snow.* Psalm 51:7

### ✳ Gather
• pattern for sled from p. 105
• pattern for lettering from pp. 106-107
• pattern for snowflake border from p. 13
• poster paper, white
• construction paper, red, green, white and black
• marker, black
• bathroom tissue roll
• string, yarn or small rope
• glue

### ✳ Prepare
Duplicate one sled each on red, green and black paper. Duplicate the lettering on green paper.

### ✳ Create
1. Post the white background paper on the bulletin board. Cut out the lettering and attach. Write the memory verse at the bottom of the board.
2. Cut and fold strips of white paper according to the instant border directions on page 10. Trace the snowflake border onto the folded paper and cut out. Staple the border around the board's edges.
3. Cut out the sleds. Cut the bathroom tissue roll into three 1½" pieces. Flatten the pieces.
4. Attach a piece of paper roll to the back of each sled.
5. Measure, cut and thread the string through each flattened roll and attach the string at an angle across the bulletin board as shown in the illustration. The students may move the sleds up and down the string while you discuss the board.

### ✳ Teach
Ask, Why do we take baths? Our memory verse asks God to wash us. But that doesn't mean that God will give us a bath like your mommy or daddy does. When God washes us, He cleans out our hearts of bad things and makes us new again, just like you take a bath to clean off the dirt. What color is snow? When God cleanses us of our bad thoughts and actions, our Bible verse says we are whiter than snow! That's very clean, isn't it? Can you think of anything that is whiter than snow? Let's thank God that our lives can be as smooth as those sleds on the string if we follow Him. Lead in a short prayer.

Suggested Usage: Winter

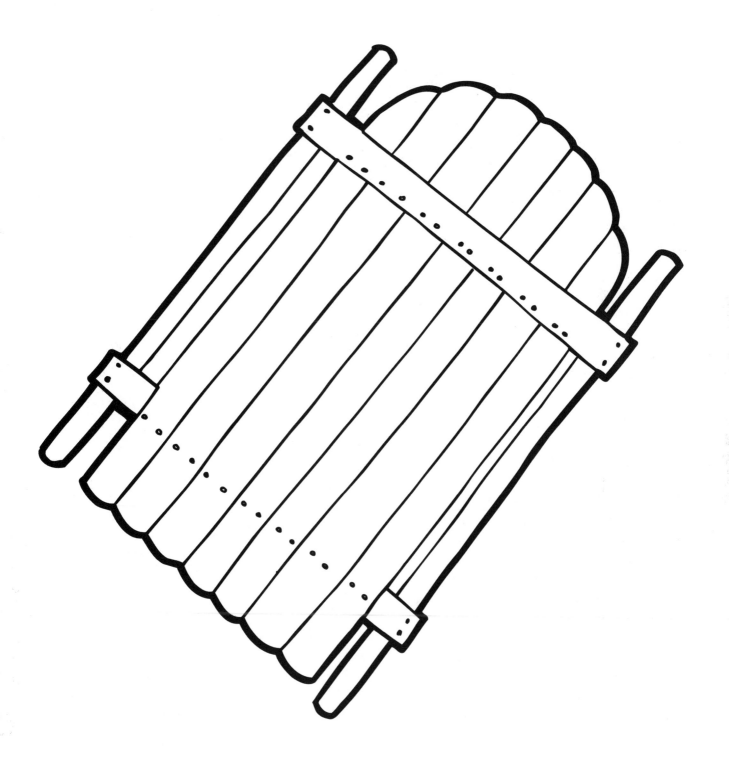

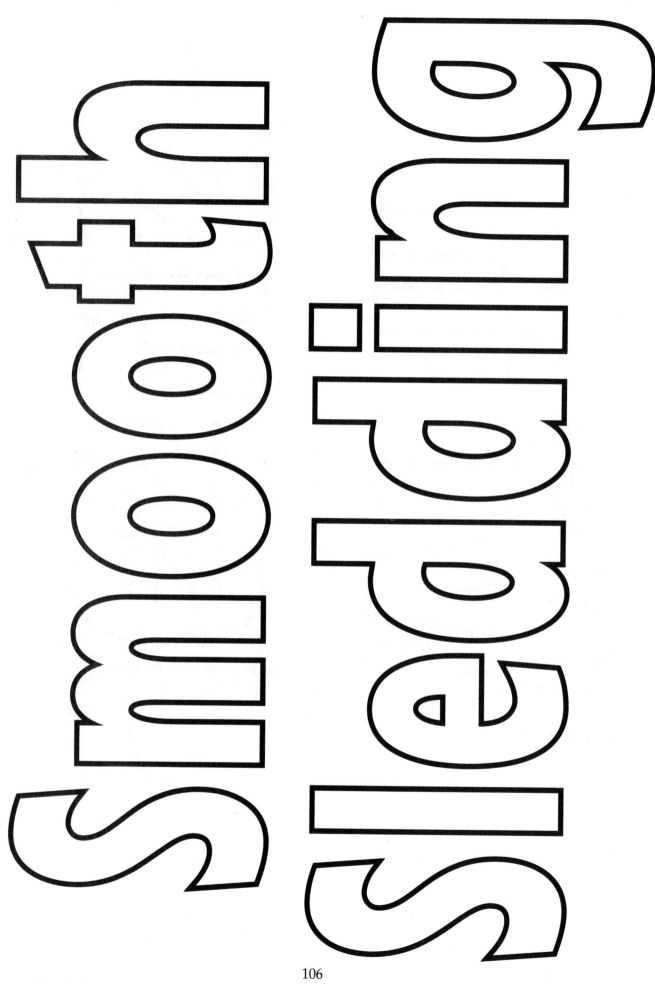

smooth

sledding

With

Jesus

## ✳ Plan

To emphasize God's plan in creation.

## ✳ Memorize

*You created my inmost being.* Psalm 139:13

## ✳ Gather

- pattern for frame from p. 109
- pattern for lettering from p. 110
- pattern for snowflake border from p. 13
- background paper, blue
- construction paper, white, red and various colors
- marker, black
- safety scissors
- crayons
- glue
- individual photos of students

## ✳ Prepare

Duplicate the lettering on red construction paper, and the frame on brown construction paper, and cut out.

## ✳ Create

1. Attach the blue background paper to the bulletin board. Cut out the lettering and attach it to the bulletin board as shown in the illustration.

2. Cut and fold strips of white construction paper according to the instant border directions on page 10. Trace the snowflake border pattern onto the folded paper and cut out the border. Staple the border around the edges of the board.

3. Have the children cut out several original snowflakes from the white construction paper using safety scissors. (To make snowflakes, fold a square piece of paper several times, cut out notches on the folds, then unfold.) Group each child's snowflakes together on the board and attach them.

4. Glue a frame over each group of snowflakes. Post the children's pictures beside their snowflakes.

## ✳ Teach

Ask, **Are any of your snowflakes the same?** Look through a few and talk about the different designs in each one. **Are any of us the same?** Look at the class and point out some differences, such as hair or eye color or the color of clothing. **God made each one of us different, just like He makes each snowflake different when it falls from the sky. We are all special because God chose to make us the way we are!**

Suggested Usage: Winter

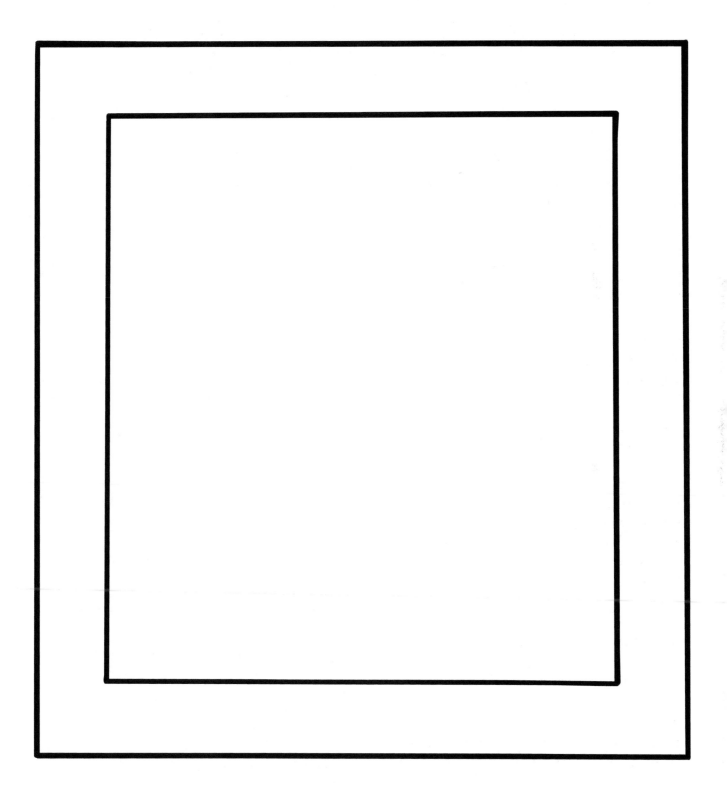

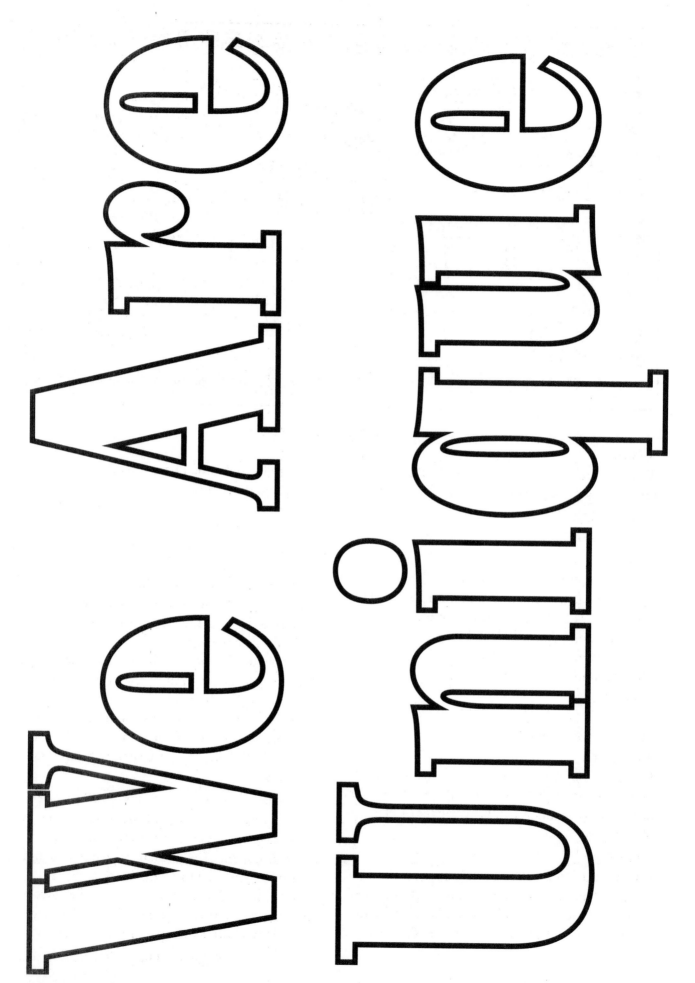

Are You a Cheerful Giver?

God loves a cheerful giver.
2 Corinthians 9:7

### ✳ Ages 6-10 ✳

### ✳ Plan
To emphasize that we should be thankful to God for everything He gives us.

### ✳ Memorize
*God loves a cheerful giver.* 2 Corinthians 9:7

### ✳ Gather
- pattern for lettering from pp. 114-115
- pattern for piggy bank and coins from pp. 112-113
- pattern for dollar sign border from p. 11
- construction paper, black and gray
- paper, white
- background paper, green
- marker, black
- crayons
- play money (optional)

### ✳ Prepare
Duplicate the lettering on black construction paper. Duplicate the piggy bank and coins on white paper, one set for each child. Cut open the slit on the top of each piggy bank.

### ✳ Create
1. Cover the bulletin board with green background paper. Cut out the lettering and attach it to the board as shown. Use a black marker to write the Bible verse at the bottom of the board.

2. Trace the dollar sign border pattern onto gray paper and cut out the border (using the instant border method from p. 10 with this pattern would create alternately backwards dollar signs). Attach the border to the board's perimeter. Or, staple play money around the board's edges.

3. Distribute a piggy bank and a coin to each student. Have each student cut out and color a bank and a coin, then write his or her name on the front of the bank.

4. Encourage the children to write some things that they could give to God on the front of their coins.

5. Staple the banks to the bulletin board, leaving their tops open. Have the students place the coins in the banks, leaving them slightly protruding.

### ✳ Teach
At the beginning of class—before working on the bulletin board—pass around a jar with pennies in it. Encourage the students to take as many as they want. Group the class in a circle, then tell them that they must share one thing for which they are thankful for each penny they took. As they give their answers, pass around the offering plate and allow them to place their pennies in the plate.

Suggested Usage: Stewardship theme

111

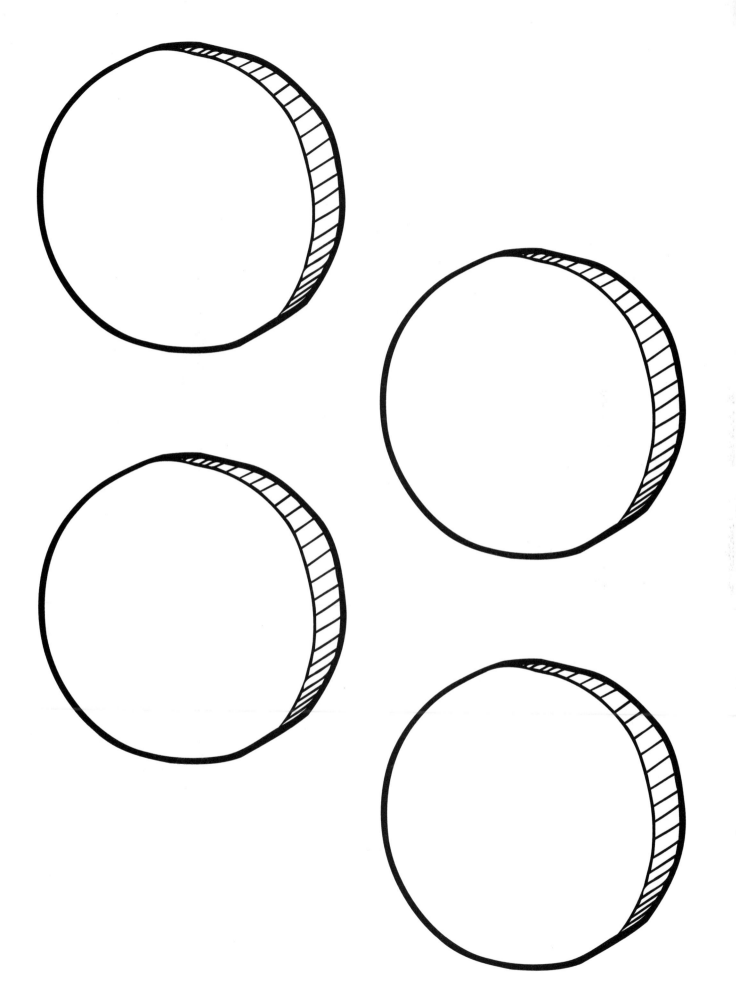

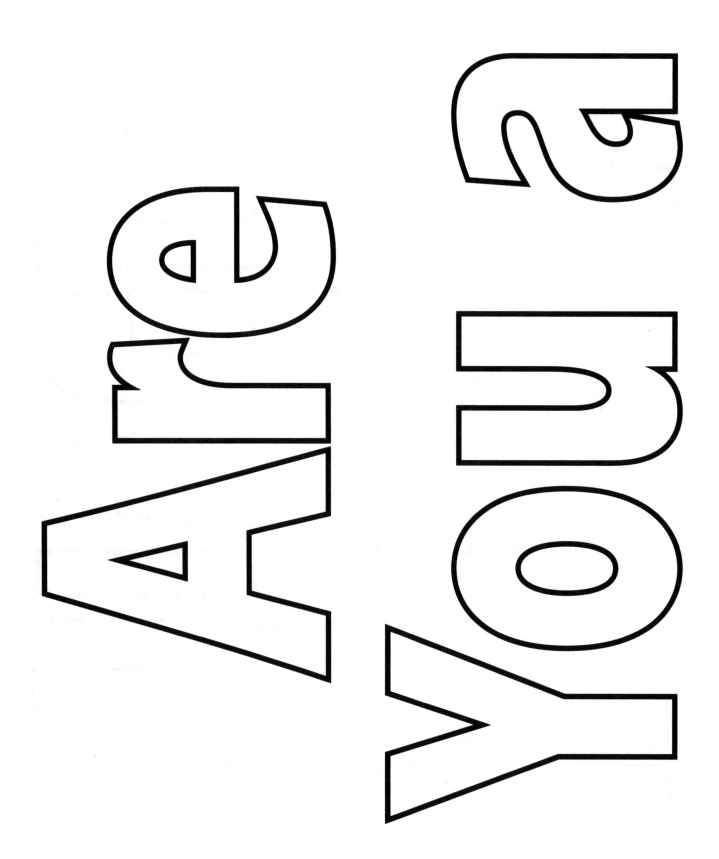

## ✳ Plan
To appreciate that God bestows gifts on us.

## ✳ Memorize
*He made a richly ornamented robe for him.*
Genesis 37:3

## ✳ Gather
• pattern for lettering from p. 118
• pattern for coat border from p. 11
• pattern for coat from p. 117
• background paper, white
• construction paper, assorted
• marker, black
• colored tissue paper, assorted
• glue
• safety scissors

## ✳ Prepare
Duplicate the lettering onto bright-colored construction paper. Duplicate one coat for each child.

## ✳ Create
1. Cover the bulletin board with white background paper. Cut out the lettering and attach it to the board as shown. Use a black marker to write the memory verse on the bottom of the board.

2. Cut and fold strips of red, yellow and blue construction paper according to the instant border directions on page 10. Trace the coat border pattern onto the folded paper and cut out the border. Post it at the board's edges for a border.

3. Distribute the coats. Have the students cut out the coats. Show how to tear bits of colored tissue or construction paper and glue them onto the coat in a patch-work pattern. You may want to prepare a sample for them to see.

4. Write the students' names on the backs of the coats. Attach the coats to the bulletin board.

## ✳ Teach
Read the story of Joseph and his coat of many colors from the Bible (Genesis, chapter 37), or from a Bible story book, before the children begin work on the bulletin board. Ask the children to share some special acts or gifts they have received from their parents. Then ask them to tell a special gift (an answer to prayer, a blessing, etc.) they received from their heavenly Father.

Suggested Usage: General

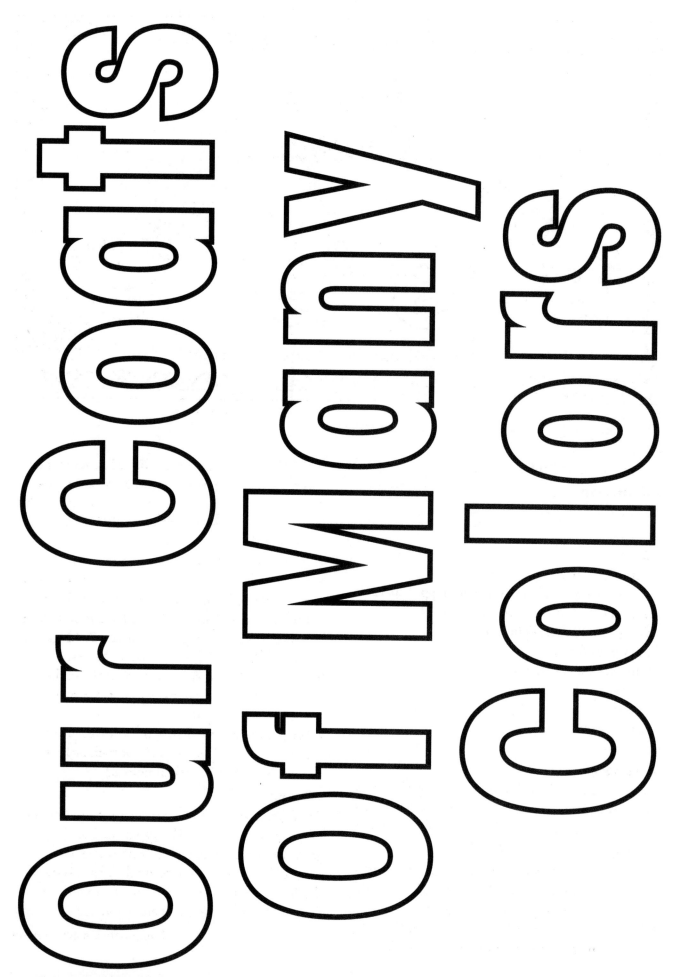

Our Coats
of Many
Colors

# Peace Makers

The fruit of righteousness will be peace. Isaiah 32:17

**✳ Ages 6-10 ✳**

## ✳ Plan
To learn about the Bible's peacemakers.

## ✳ Memorize
*The fruit of righteousness will be peace.*
Isaiah 32:17

## ✳ Gather
• pattern for lettering from p. 122
• pattern for dove and olive leaves from pp. 120-121
• pattern for olive leaf border from p. 12
• background paper, light blue
• aluminum foil
• construction paper, white and green
• marker, black
• Velcro
• plastic sandwich bag
• push pin

## ✳ Prepare
Trace the lettering on aluminum foil. Duplicate six doves on white paper, and six small olive leaves and one large olive leaf on green paper.

## ✳ Create
1. Cover the board with light blue paper. Cut out the lettering and attach it to the board. Write the Bible verse at the bottom of the board.
2. Cut and fold strips of green paper according to the instant border directions on page 10. Trace the olive leaf border on the folded paper and cut out. Staple the border around the board's edges.
3. Cut out the doves. On each one, write one of the "Who Am I?" questions from p. 102. Attach the doves to the bulletin board.
4. Place a piece of Velcro next to each dove's beak.
5. Cut out the olive leaves. On each small leaf, write one of the following: Jonathan, Abigail, Jesus, Esther, Joseph, Moses. On the large leaf, make an answer key by writing: 1. Jonathan; 2. Abigail; 3. Jesus; 4. Esther; 5. Joseph; and 6. Moses.
6. Stick the other halves of Velcro on the backs of the small leaves. Store the leaves in a plastic bag pinned to the board.
7. Invite the students to match the leaves to the correct doves. Have them check their answers with the answer key when finished.

## ✳ Teach
Review each of the Bible stories represented by the questions and answers. Then split the class into groups and assign each group with one of the stories. The groups must devise their own ways of acting out their stories using only pantomime for the rest of the class to guess and name.

Suggested Usage: General

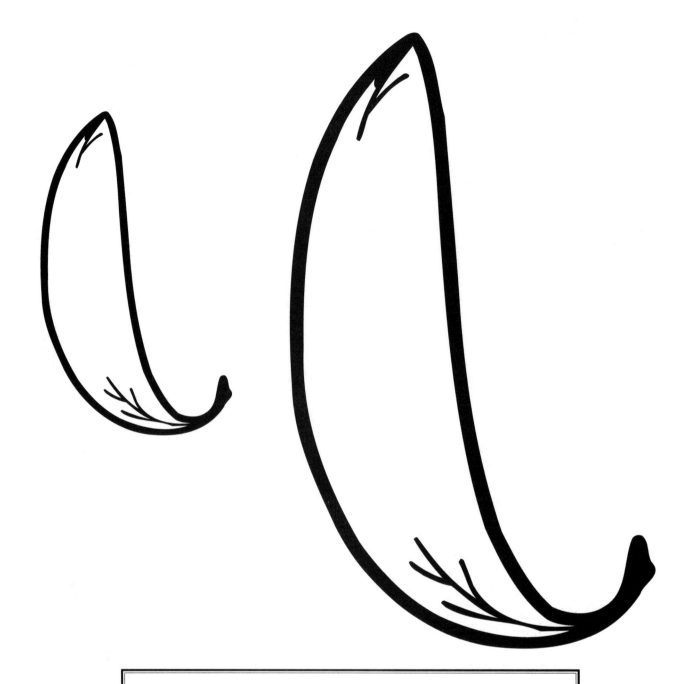

### "Who Am I?" Questions for "Peace Makers"

1. I warned my best friend, David, about my father's plan to kill him. Who am I?

2. I prepared bread, meat and fruit for King David's soldiers when my husband Nabal refused. Who am I?

3. I am known as the Lord of Peace. Who am I?

4. I went to King Xerxes about Haman's plan to kill Jewish people. Who am I?

5. My brothers sold me into slavery. But I forgave them. Who am I?

6. I went to Pharoah many times, asking him to let my people go. Who am I?

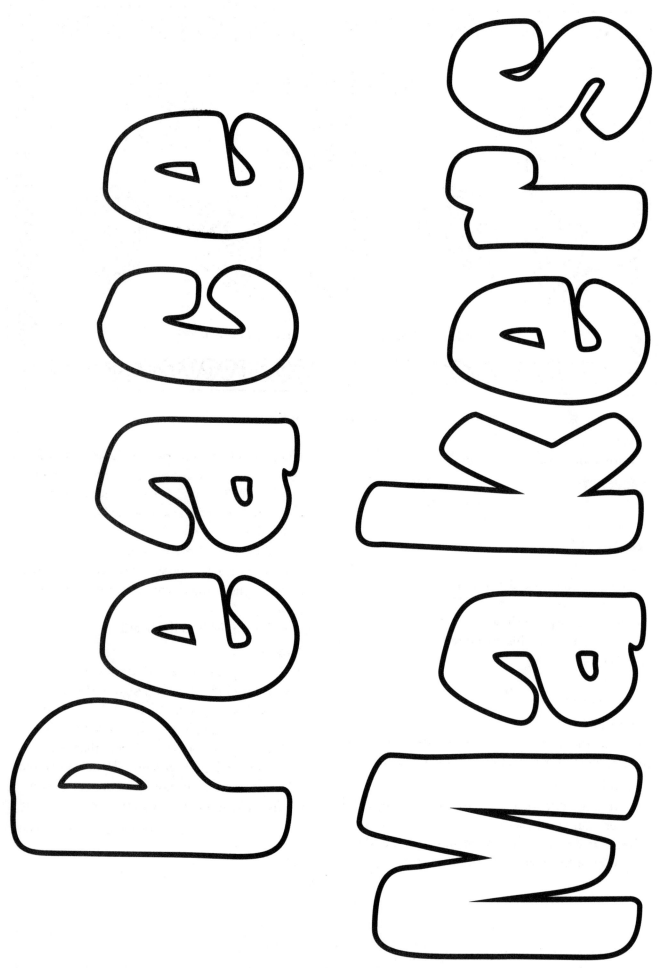

# Shields Of Faith

*He is a shield to those whose walk is blameless. Proverbs 2:7*

## ✴ Ages 6-10 ✴

### ✴ Plan
To learn about God's care for us.

### ✴ Memorize
*He is a shield to those whose walk is blameless.*
Proverbs 2:7

### ✴ Gather
• pattern for shield from p. 124
• pattern for shield border from p. 13
• pattern for lettering from p. 125
• background paper, yellow
• construction paper, black and red
• marker, black
• crayons
• safety scissors

### ✴ Prepare
Duplicate the lettering on black construction paper, and one shield for each student on white paper.

### ✴ Create
1. Cover the bulletin board with yellow background paper. Cut out the lettering and attach it to the board as shown. Write the memory verse at the bottom of the board with a black marker.

2. Cut strips of red construction paper and fold them according to the instant border directions on page 10. Trace the shield border pattern on the folded paper and cut out the border. Post the shield border around the board's edges.

3. Distribute the shields to the students. Have them cut out the shields and use crayons to make their own designs, using a symbol to represent themselves.

4. Attach the shields to the board.

### ✴ Teach
Before starting this project, discuss with the students the historical use and design of shields (an encyclopedia or other reference book is helpful and has illustrated examples). Tell how families had shields with special designs on them that were unique to their family surname. Then explain that God is like a shield for those who believe in Him, and His shield is for anyone in the Christian family.

Suggested Usage: General

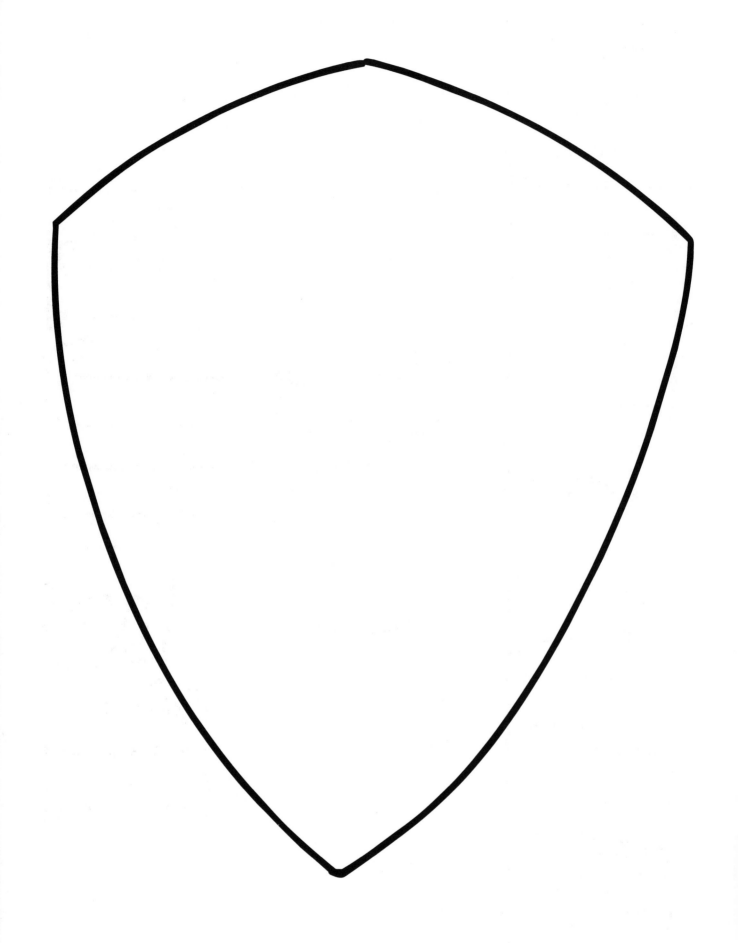

Shields

of

Faith

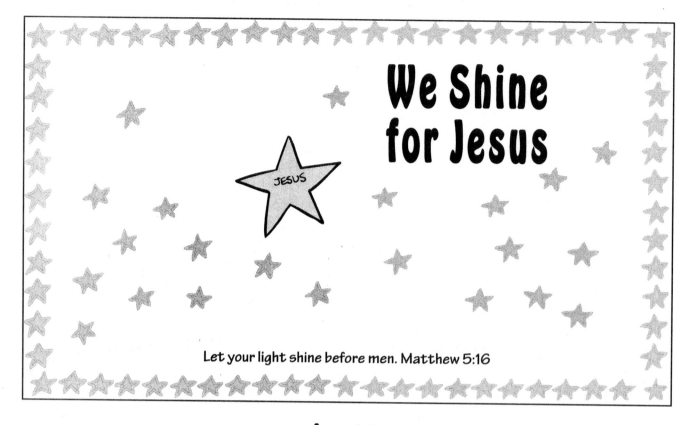

**We Shine for Jesus**

JESUS

Let your light shine before men. Matthew 5:16

**❋ Plan**

To explain how Christians are instructed to show God's love.

**❋ Memorize**

*Let your light shine before men.* Matthew 5:16

**❋ Gather**

- pattern for large star from p. 127
- pattern for lettering from p. 128
- pattern for star border from p. 13
- poster board, white
- background paper, blue
- construction paper, yellow
- aluminum foil
- craft paint pens
- Velcro
- marker, black
- sunglasses

**❋ Prepare**

Duplicate the lettering on yellow paper. Cut out one large star from white poster board using the pattern, then use the star border pattern on page 13 to cut out one poster board star for each child.

**❋ Create**

1. Attach the blue background paper to the board. Cut out the lettering and attach it to the board. Write the memory verse at the bottom.

2. Cut and fold strips of yellow paper according to the instant border directions on page 10. Trace the star border onto the folded paper and cut out. Staple the border around the board's edges.

3. Cover the stars with aluminum foil. Write "Jesus" on the large star with the craft paint pen and attach the star to the board.

4. Write a child's name on each little star. Attach a small piece of Velcro to the back of each little star and to the bulletin board.

5. The children may remove and replace their stars on the board. You may use this bulletin board as an attendance chart by having the children post their stars each time they are present.

**❋ Teach**

Bring a pair of sunglasses but keep them hidden. Ask, **Are we able to see the stars shining at night even though the sky is dark? Jesus says that when we love Him we should shine like the stars. How can we shine? Let's practice being shiny.** Sing praise songs or go around the room and have each child say something positive. As the children get involved in "shiny" acts, pull out your sunglasses, put them on, and say, **Oh, you are so shiny already that I can barely see!** Continue "blocking the glare" as the children act out their shiny behavior.

Suggested Usage: General

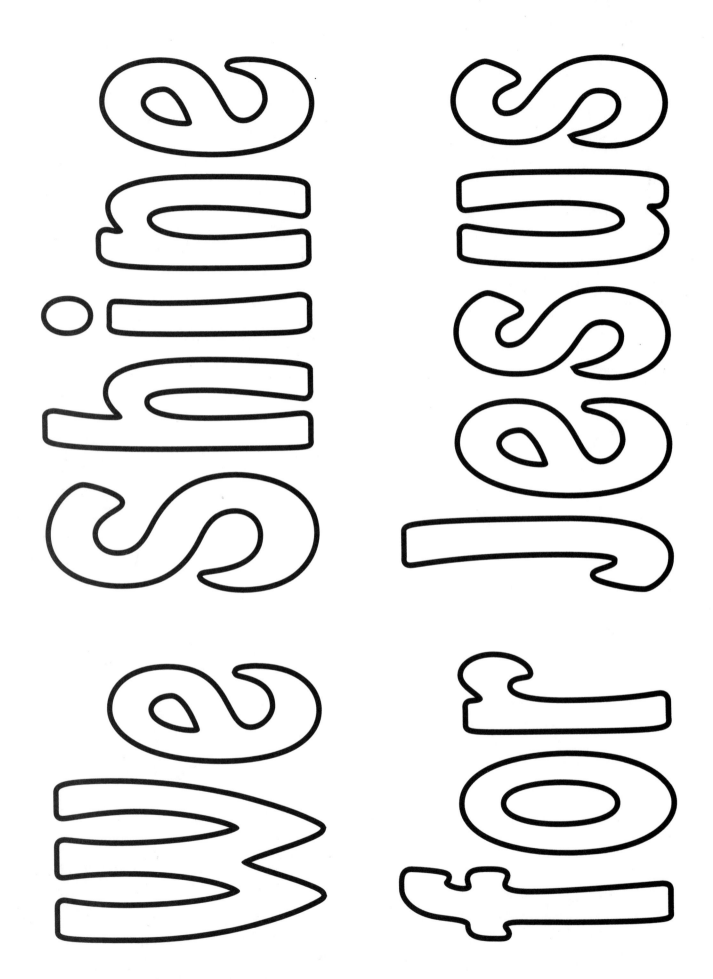